CHARTING YOUR COURSE: How to Prepare to Teach More Effectively

BY RICHARD PRÉGENT

CENTER FOR TEACHING AND LEARNING,
ÉCOLE POLYTECHNIQUE DE MONTRÉAL
UNIVERSITÉ DE MONTRÉAL

Atwood Publishing
Madison, Wisconsin

Charting Your Course
How to Prepare to Teach More Effectively
by Richard Prégent

Cover design by TLC Graphics, www.TLCGraphics.com

ISBN: 2-533-000216-3

Library of Congress Cataloging-in-Publication Data

Prégent, Richard, 1950-
[Préparation d'un cours. English]
Charting your course: how to prepare to teach more effectively/ by Richard Prégent.
p. cm.
Includes bibliographical references and index.
ISBN 1-891859-06-4
1. College teaching. 2. Education, Higher—Curricula. 3. Lesson planning. I. Title.

LB2331 .P6813 2000
378.1'2—dc21

00-056606

Atwood Publishing
2710 Atwood Ave.
Madison, WI 53704
888/242-7101
www.atwoodpublishing.com

TO MY FATHER, DOMINA PRÉGENT

／
ACKNOWLEDGMENTS

This work would never have come into being without the invaluable collaboration of several professors at the École Polytechnique of Montréal who allowed me to use and adapt some real examples in several chapters.

People from other universities also contributed generously to this work through their critical reading and commentaries, which I greatly appreciate.

Thus I would like very much to express my gratitude to this entire group of people: Patrick Babin, Huguette Bernard, Louise Boisvert, Chantal Bouthat, Carole Burney-Vincent, Dominique Chassé, Yves Comeau, Aline Côté, France Cormier, Jean Dansereau, Paul Grand'Maison, Chahé Nerguizian, Michel Prud'Homme, Denis Rouleau, Bernard Sanschagrin, Guy Savoie, Rolland Viau, Robert Vinet, and Charles Widmer.

I would particularly like to thank Jean Dulude, Director of the Pedagogical Service of the École Polytechnique of Montréal, for his unfailing encouragement and support.

Moreover, a dynamic and competent production team helped me edit and publish this text. For the original French language volume, my thanks go first to Lucie Presseault, who collaborated closely on entering the text. They go as well to Louise Régnier, who was in charge of publishing this work. I must also mention the diligent efforts of Jean-Claude Poupard, who proofread my work. Finally, I thank Daniel Viens, Chantal Fauteux, and Bénédicte Stordeur for their meticulous care in graphic conception and electronic production.

For the English language volume, I thank Marcia Parker, who translated the work. Further, I wish to thank Robert Magnan and Linda Babler, who edited and designed the English version.

FOREWORD

This work is addressed to all professors and teaching assistants who will at some time have to prepare a new course. To help them accomplish this task, I have decided to give them the benefit of my experience as a consultant in higher education by proposing a systematic approach to course preparation.

This approach is universal, since it applies to all disciplines and to regular courses, intensive courses, or lectures.

This approach, the bases of which have existed for about 40 years, is most familiar to academics, as it is related to the classic approach to problem-solving. It requires, before any action, a global analysis of the situation; it then demands thought, planning, and methodical preparation; finally, it entails an evaluation of the results.

I have tested this approach for 10 years with hundreds of professors and in dozens of courses, principally in engineering. The professors who have applied it always have been highly satisfied with it; they have particularly appreciated the advantages of its systematic nature, the feeling of mastering course preparation without forgetting anything, and their increased confidence in accomplishing a task whose outcome sometimes seemed uncertain to them.

Although the approach I propose is classic, what I present here is unique. I propose concrete and flexible recommendations, methods, and instruments, simple scenarios, and practical suggestions that I have refined over more than a decade of consultation. I also provide several examples of work produced with the help of these instruments.

Furthermore, what is unique is the synthetic aspect of this guide: it covers, in a reasonable number of pages, numerous concepts of college and university teaching — concepts that faculty members could otherwise discover only through reading much longer, specialized works. This text, although it does not replace complementary readings, offers an appreciable shortcut, allowing professors to make their way rapidly and easily through the maze of jargon and concepts of postsecondary pedagogy, so that they can prepare any course systematically.

Richard Prégent

TABLE OF CONTENTS

Chapter 4

Choosing Your Teaching Methods

Chapter 5

Choosing Your Teaching Materials

Chapter 6

Detailed Course Planning

INTRODUCTION

The procedure I propose for preparing a new course covers nine chapters, which describe chronological processes. This linear procedure is handy, even if it does not totally do justice to the nature of the task of designing and preparing a new course. Course preparation is actually a *systemic procedure* in which we must often think simultaneously of the interaction of several aspects.

The procedure I propose consists of a certain number of operations, as presented in Figure I.1 (on the following page). The text generally follows the chronology of these operations, although we regroup some of them.

In Chapter 1, I recommend that you clearly examine the conditions of the teaching situation that you have inherited. You must analyze the events that have led to creation of the course, compare the scope of the work to be accomplished with the resources and time at your disposal, identify the characteristics of your students, and adapt the course content to their needs.

In Chapter 2, I recommend that you *formulate your course objectives*. I attempt to simplify and demystify the formulation of objectives, and I stress their fundamental role in all subsequent operations. This chapter also covers the different levels of objectives.

In Chapter 3, I enter into *planning how to evaluate learning*. I first examine the two roles that evaluation may play: summative and formative. I then describe several evaluation instruments and provide criteria for choosing them. Finally, I give practical advice on developing, administering, and correcting exams.

In Chapter 4, I describe, almost exhaustively, the *teaching methods* that allow you to help your students attain the course objectives. Here again, I provide some selection criteria.

In Chapter 5, I list *teaching materials* and analyze the relative pedagogical impact of these materials. I also give practical advice on correctly using each type of material.

Figure I.1 Operations Necessary for Systematic Course Preparation

Analyzing:

1. the conditions of the teaching situation...*Chapter 1*
2. the characteristics of the students...*Chapter 1*
3. the course content...*Chapter 1*

Planning:

4. the course objectives...*Chapter 2*
5. evaluation of the students...*Chapter 3*
6. the choice of teaching methods...*Chapter 4*
7. the choice of teaching materials...*Chapter 5*
8. the course outline...*Chapter 6*
9. the course syllabus...*Chapter 6*
10. the lesson plan...*Chapter 6*

Conducting:

11. the course according to preparation
    -using lectures...*Chapter 7*
    -using group work...*Chapter 8*

Evaluating:

12. the course at midterm...*Chapter 9*
13. the course at the end of the term...*Chapter 9*

In Chapter 6, I enter into *detailed planning of different learning activities*, using the course syllabus, the course outline, and the lesson plan.

In Chapter 7, I consider the most widespread teaching method, *the lecture*. I first suggest a series of useful operations to prepare the explanations for a presentation. I then present a general model for lectures. (Throughout this book, I use the terms "explanation" and "explaining" as defined and used by George Brown in *Lecturing and Explaining* (p. 7): "Put simply, explaining is giving understanding to someone else.")

In Chapter 8, I describe *how to help students work better in groups*. I first explain how to divide the energy in a good work group and how to hold effective meetings. I then suggest a strategy for training students to work in groups, using a number of exercises throughout the term.

In Chapter 9, I propose two means of *formatively evaluating your teaching*, the first around midterm and the second at the end of the term.

Two Useful Tips

Before entering into the procedure for systematic course preparation, I would like to offer two recommendations to help you avoid the following two errors frequently made in preparing a new course: wanting to do everything at once and forgetting that a course should be for students.

First tip: Don't try to do everything the first time.

It is better to plan to finalize a course in two years, even three years, and then start by determining what is essential for the first time: content, methods, and materials.

This certainly does not mean that you don't need to do the best job possible the first time. However, it's unrealistic to think that you can develop, in a few months, all the resources that you would wish for a new course.

Developing a new course should not take all of your energy; you must be able to continue with your other teaching tasks, research, publication, and other duties. Too often professors wear themselves out creating a new course, to the point of affecting their other professional and personal activities. A happy medium is necessary if you want to enjoy teaching a course that has taken so much work to prepare.

That's why we must imagine a new course as a work in progress; however logical and systematic the initial design, a new course always requires adjustments. Moreover, a professor who has put too much energy into preparing the first version of a new course may not easily accept making adjustments, because the course may seem to have already taken enough effort. On the other hand, a professor who has planned to develop a new course progressively is more likely to find it normal to make adjustments and integrate them into the development plan.

To teach a new course for the first time, then, you should plan for a design that is more sure than original, with objectives more modest than ambitious, and resources more simple than complex. In brief, count on progressively developing all aspects of the course as a whole rather than on definitively perfecting each of these aspects.

Second tip: Don't forget that a course must be conceived and prepared for the students, not the professor.

For the professor whose sole concern is *teaching*, preparing a new course amounts to preparing lectures and tests. On the other hand, for the professor concerned about *helping students learn*, the work also involves preparing a host of other pedagogical activities for the students.

Certain activities will give students the opportunity to verify, in class or elsewhere, their comprehension of the material; others will allow them to apply what they think they have understood; still others will help them to sharpen their sense of analysis, synthesis, and critical judgment concerning the course material.

As strange as it may appear to some, the professor must not be the center of attraction in the course. On the contrary, the students must play the leading roles, under the direction of the professor.

When you picture your role in that way, you feel liberated from the weight of the course, because it's no longer up to you to prove, through your lectures, that you really know the course material. Rather, it's up to the students to put forth the effort to master this material.

You then become a "knowledge engineer"; you determine what the students must learn. You plan and evaluate the activities and materials through which your students attain the objectives you have set. You prepare remedial activities whenever appropriate. You motivate your students, like the leader in a professional work group.

In brief, plan to play a much more complex role than simply dispensing knowledge.

CHAPTER 1

ANALYZING THE CONDITIONS OF YOUR TEACHING SITUATION

In this chapter, I will first show that analyzing the context for creating a course (that is, analyzing certain events past, present, or future) can furnish information that will influence your preparation.

Next, you will see that certain student characteristics, notably their academic profile and expectations, can also influence your course preparation.

Finally, I propose a general, systematic six-step approach to help you analyze and determine the subject content of a new course. You will see that this analysis helps you determine how to organize your course subjects and how much time to allot to each, as well as how to choose a textbook.

1.1 Context of Course Creation

Before preparing a new course, you must know the conditions of your teaching situation. You must know in what circumstances the course was approved (the past). You must also know the time limits imposed, as well as the financial conditions and the resources at your disposal (the present). Finally, you must know the pedagogical conditions under which you will teach the course (the future).

1.1.1 Past

In order to determine the circumstances under which the course was approved, you must try to answer the following questions:

- Who approved the new course?
- What official needs is the course to fulfill?
- Were there special reasons to create this course?

Generally, department, faculty, or campus authorities approve a new course. You can learn the underlying motives for the new course by talking with the appropriate authorities or by reading official documents relating to this course. You can then identify the fundamental needs that this course should fulfill. Incidentally, you can also discover what special reasons may be behind this course.

The usual reasons for creating a course are often the necessity:

- to meet the needs of the labor market;
- to satisfy the requirements of a national accreditation organism;
- to update old content;
- to respond to important developments in a modern field.

But very often, in creating a new course, authorities have secondary objectives as well. Thus, among other goals, they may want to use this course to improve the quality of laboratories in a department, encourage professors to computerize the assignments they give, or simply compete with another college or university.

Therefore, it is better to know all of these official and unofficial reasons before beginning to prepare a new course.

1.1.2 Present

Before launching into the preparation of a new course, you must evaluate:

- the extent of work involved in this preparation;
- the resources at your disposal.

The time necessary to prepare a new course is directly proportional to the number of tasks required to complete preparation.

Each course is different and unique. Depending on the circumstances, it may require one or more of the following tasks:

- updating knowledge relating to the course material;
- research, travel, and meetings with colleagues;
- holding organizational meetings;
- fine-tuning laboratories, assignments, exercises, and discussion sections;
- drafting a course plan, handouts, lab session guides, and project guides;
- integrating or adapting computer software to the course or to assignments;
- training technicians, teaching assistants, and graders;
- drafting specific lesson plans;
- preparing transparencies or other audio-visual-scipto materials;
- coordinating the tasks of several professors;
- developing exams, answer keys, and grading scales.

Organizing and synchronizing all of these tasks requires that you realistically evaluate the time required relative to the time available.

You must also analyze your other constraints and take inventory of the material, financial, and human resources at your disposal.

You must take into account the deadline by which the course is to be prepared (in a month, a semester, or a year) and certain other useful data:

facilities available (such as an office and computer) budget to buy books and hire students or specialists for support, etc.

Most professors work alone and have relatively few resources available to prepare a new course. Others enjoy more extensive budgetary and human resources. However, easy access to numerous resources increases the need for planning and coordinating time, resources, and collaborators. You must, therefore, also realistically evaluate whether such a pedagogical undertaking is compatible with the time you have available.

1.1.3 Future

In preparing a new course, you must also assess the conditions under which you will be teaching. You must determine:

- the anticipated enrollment;
- whether or not the course is required;
- how many semesters you will teach this course;
- what rooms, equipment, laboratories, and staff you will have.

It's also essential to know the approximate number of students who are going to enroll in the course before you prepare it.

For example, with a class of about 20 students, you can easily plan any pedagogical activity: lectures, discussions, group work, seminars, case studies, projects, laboratories, visits, or other activities.

On the other hand, the situation will be different with a group of 40 to 60 students. It will be even more different if the students number 100, 300, 500, or even 1,000, divided into sections with professors whose activities will have to be coordinated.

In fact, the larger the group, the more detailed your preparation must be and the more you must know about the resources available.

If the course is an elective, you can expect students to be motivated. Your work will therefore, be easier. On the other hand, if the course is required, you will probably need to make a special effort to stimulate and motivate the students.

Moreover, you must try to find out how long the course will be offered. If there is an extensive commitment (several semesters or several years), you are more likely to invest much more time in preparation. In contrast, if the course will be offered only one semester, you might invest less effort — which is understandable, because, here as elsewhere, your effort must be proportional to the return.

Depending on the nature of the course to be prepared, you might feel a need for special resources: rooms, equipment, technicians, assistants, or graders. If these resources are not available, you will have to moderate your ambitions and take these constraints into account in your planning.

1.2 Student Characteristics

For a message to be effective, it must be expressed in terms that correspond to the level of comprehension and interests of the target audience. In brief, the more appropriately a message is expressed, the more likely it is to be effective.

It is for these reasons that we advise you to analyze the characteristics of the students likely to enroll in your course.

If you identify the abilities, knowledge, and interests of these students, you can design a course more specifically adapted to them.

Of course, since this analysis is theoretical, you cannot be 100% confident. However, the risk of being radically mistaken is minimal.

In this analysis, you should bear in mind two principal factors:

- the academic profile of the students;
- their motives for enrolling in the course.

1.2.1 Academic Profile

To obtain the academic profile of the students interested in enrolling in a new course, you must try to determine:

- the students' schools, departments, or disciplines;
- the nature of their programs and the courses they have taken;
- the content and pedagogical organization of the previous courses;
- the degree of homogeneity of the enrolling students;
- the requirements of subsequent courses.

Most of this information is available in the bulletins of the different schools or departments. However, since information collected in this way is theoretical, you should contact the office of the registrar, or colleagues responsible for the previous courses, to obtain more concrete information on the academic background of the students you expect to teach. You can examine the course outlines (which generally give the objectives) the detailed contents of the course and lab sessions, the list of assignments, the list of required textbooks, and bibliographies.

All of this information will allow you to choose course objectives and a pedagogical organization matching your students' level of comprehension.

Analyzing characteristics of the student body in general also allows you to determine whether the group of students you are going to meet will be homogeneous or heterogeneous, in terms of development, knowledge, and experience.

When the group is homogeneous (for example, students coming from the same program), course preparation is easier, because you can plan explanations, terms, examples, and references at the same level.

On the other hand, when you prepare a course for a heterogeneous group, as is now very common, you must consider that you will have to continually adapt your approaches to the diverse student profiles. You must plan explanations, examples, and so forth of varying nature and difficulty. Throughout the course, you will regularly have to verify whether the pace is appropriate, and you will have to be ready to adapt to different levels of comprehension: for some students, the course might be too easy; for others, it will be too difficult.

Finally, in preparing a new course, you must also be aware of the education required for subsequent courses. To find out the requirements for these courses, you can use the approach recommended above for analyzing the academic profiles of the students and determining the contents of previous courses: read bulletins, meet with colleagues, analyze course plans, and analyze exams.

With these techniques, you can better define your teaching responsibilities and avoid useless duplication of work in the courses that precede or follow the one you are preparing.

1.2.2 Expectations

In general, when students enroll in a course, they have certain hopes and expectations for the course. If they notice from the start that their expectations will probably be fulfilled, their participation and intellectual commitment are bound to be established. If not, disappointment and apathy can set in for a certain time, or even for the rest of the course.

You should, therefore, find out about the expectations of your students and try to answer these questions:

- What are their professional expectations for the course?

- What are their personal expectations for the course?
- Do the students know each other, and have they worked together previously?

It is relatively easy to define professional expectations — that is, how students hope to benefit in the course of their careers from the knowledge they acquire in the course. You can thus easily identify content or applications that attract students on the professional level, by referring to your own experience and underscoring it through concrete examples.

On the other hand, it is more difficult to identify students' personal motivations. To do so properly, it would be necessary to interview a sample of the future students. Unfortunately, that is difficult. However, you can question colleagues who have already taught these students and discover, for example, that these students expect either a practical or a theoretical course, or that they hope to do a project, or that they expect either an overview of numerous subjects or an intensive treatment of some of these subjects.

Though you know these expectations, you are not obligated to fulfill all of them. Rather, you will have to prioritize them. Doing so will result in guidelines permitting you to qualify your decisions concerning the choice of content, assignments or projects, and documentary resources. If you actually take into account the expectations your students have for the course, you will increase the chances of commitment and active participation.

Moreover, you should not forget that the students will constitute a group when they gather in your class. Therefore, you must try to identify the level of cohesion or solidarity of this group before making certain decisions about the pedagogical organization of the course (e.g., organization of group work, Chapter 8).

On the one hand, if the students know each other, you will be able to take advantage of the energy generated by the solidarity and simply lead the group already formed.

On the other hand, if the students do not know each other, you will have to work to create conditions to promote solidarity. Students are not robots with the power to participate spontaneously; they are human beings who, like all of us, need to adapt before accepting or participating fully in a learning activity or group activities. This is a crucial task that you must accomplish if you want to encourage students who do not know each other to participate in group activities.

1.3 Course Content

Establishing the content of a new course is a different task for each professor. If you are a specialist in the area of the new course, you can analyze and determine the content of the course quickly, because your knowledge and experience considerably helps you accomplish this task.

On the other hand, if you must teach a subject relatively foreign to your specialty, you must do research, even extensively, before analyzing the subject material and the content.

In any case, it is your responsibility to choose the content of a new course by reflecting on the importance, difficulty, and organization of each of the different themes and subjects you intend to present.

We suggest that you follow six steps in analyzing the subject material and establishing the content of a new course:

1. Identify all of the themes that seem relevant;
2. List all of the subjects that constitute each theme;
3. Assess the importance and difficulty of each subject listed;
4. Choose the subjects to treat, using a decision matrix;
5. Determine the order and time to allot for the selected subjects;
6. Choose the textbook.

The order of these tasks is not rigid; in reality, some of these tasks can be reversed or simultaneous. This, however, is an order that seems logical, and we will use it to describe these six tasks in greater detail.

1.3.1 Identifying Possible Themes

You can start by brainstorming to identify all of the possible themes that seem relevant to the course. Don't limit yourself at this point; it's best to be productive and imaginative and list all of the themes that come to mind. In addition, you must defer judgment about the relevance of each of these themes; that task comes later.

1.3.2 Listing Possible Subjects for Each Theme

We then recommend that for each theme you make the most exhaustive list possible of all of the subjects constituting this theme, again avoiding judgment of their relevance. You will then have a more complete overview of the subjects you could tackle in your course if time were not a constraint.

In order not to overlook anything, you should also consult the table of contents of reputable books in the subject area of the course, course bulletins from other institutions, or course outlines developed by colleagues who teach similar courses elsewhere.

1.3.3 Assessing the Importance and Difficulty of Each Subject Listed

Before choosing which subjects to treat — and in order to do so more objectively — you should assess the degree of importance and difficulty of each of them.

Degree of Importance. This first assessment allows you to rate the importance that you ascribe to each one of the subjects you have listed. To do so, you can use any scale of values you choose, such as the one proposed below:

- Not very important. . . . .1 point
- Important. . . . . 2 points
- Very important. . . . . 3 points

Degree of Difficulty. This second assessment permits you to estimate the presumed difficulty for students to understand and assimilate each of the subjects listed. Again, you can use any scale of values. For example:

- Easy. . . . .1 point
- Difficult. . . . . 2 points
- Very difficult. . . . . 3 points

1.3.4 Choosing Subjects Using a Decision Matrix

By using a decision matrix to group the ratings assigned to each subject of importance and difficulty, you can choose the subjects for your course more objectively. Table 1.1 below gives a theoretical example of this procedure. The final choice of subjects is a question of judgment and compromise, of course. However, the following basic principles should guide you:

Table 1.1 Decision Matrix

Theme and subjects	Level of importance	Level of difficulty
Theme A		
subject *x*	3	2
subject *y*	2	1
subject *z*	2	2
Theme B		
subject *x*	1	1
subject *y*	1	3
subject *z*	3	2

- First select the *essential* subjects. At the outset, allot them more time than you allot to the *subjects that are important but not essential.*
- Then, within each category of subjects, allot more time to the subjects considered *very difficult.*

1.3.5 Determining the Order and Time Allotment for the Chosen Subjects

It is almost impossible, and even presumptuous, to suggest one single approach to determine the order for covering subjects in a new course. Each course can require a particular sequence that is logical in one case but not in another. It is up to you, for each course, to determine to the best of your knowledge the "ideal" order — which you can revise as appropriate after a semester of experience.

You must next allocate approximate time allotments for each of the selected subjects. At this stage, you should allot time in hours rather than minutes — for example, two hours for subject x, five hours for subject y, and so forth, the total obviously not exceeding the overall length of the course.

It is only when you plan the course syllabus and prepare the lesson plans (Chapter 6) that you will be able to determine progressively the exact amount of time to allot to each subject selected.

1.3.6 Choosing the Textbook

Finally, and with full knowledge of the facts, you can choose the textbook, which should, of course, reflect the logic and choices of the preceding steps.

If the treatment of the subject matter in a given textbook agrees with your views, the choice becomes easy. It is even quite likely that the order of subjects will be more or less close to the one that you have established.

On the other hand, if no textbook deals significantly with the subjects that you have selected, or if you wish to synthesize several textbooks, the choice becomes difficult, because it is inappropriate to require students to buy three or four textbooks. In this case, you should consider combining a textbook that covers at least 50% to 60% of the content of your course with complementary handouts that you will compile for the rest of the content.

You may even choose to compile a complete set of handouts — with an organized text and illustrations — in which you will choose an original and personal structure and approach to the course content.

Remember, however, that compiling a handout can require several hundred hours of work, and that it's certainly not wise to devote too much effort to preparing a handout and too little to the other stages of preparing a new course.

If you have little time to prepare a new course, you should take a less original, but realistic approach to materials the first time you teach the course. In some cases, it might be better to choose a textbook that does not meet all of your needs perfectly. Or you could use an outline handout (a sort of detailed table of contents) that will permit students to take notes in class. You could even distribute copies of the transparencies you use during the course, so that students can supplement them with notes from class or readings.

In fact, developing a voluminous handout is very often a task that is wise to defer or spread out over several years.

Review

Content of Course Creation

Past

- Who approved the new course?
- What official and unofficial needs is the course to fulfill?
- Were there special reasons to create this course?

Present

- What is the extent of work involved in preparing the new course?
- What resources are at your disposal?

Future

- What is the anticipated enrollment for the course?
- Is the course required?
- For how many semesters will the course be offered?
- Are rooms, equipment, laboratories, and support staff available?

Student Characteristics

Academic profile

- What are the students' schools, departments, or disciplines?
- What is the nature of their programs and the curriculum they have followed?
- What are the content and pedagogical organization of their previous courses?
- What is the degree of homogeneity of the enrolling students?
- What are the requirements of subsequent courses?

Expectations

- What professional expectations do students have for the course?
- What personal expectations do students have for the course?
- Do the students in the course know each other? Have they worked together previously?

Course Content

Steps in analyzing the subject material and establishing course content:

1. Identify all of the themes that seem relevant.
2. List all of the subjects that constitute each theme.
3. Assess the importance and difficulty of each subject listed.
4. Choose the subjects to treat, using a decision matrix.
5. Determine the order and time allotment for the chosen subjects.
6. Choose the textbook.

CHAPTER 2

FORMULATING COURSE OBJECTIVES

Although the list of subjects you establish constitutes a good planning tool, it does not allow you to identify the actions students will be able to accomplish by the end of the course, nor their level of performance. You can accurately determine these aspects by formulating course objectives.

In this chapter, we first define the two principal types of pedagogical objectives: general and specific. (Authors of other works on learning objectives propose a more complex hierarchy — ends, goals, general, specific, terminal, and intermediate objectives. We will keep our presentation simple, dealing only with *general objectives* and *specific objectives*.)

Next we demonstrate that formulating objectives is a progressive process that moves from general to specific.

After that, we show how to draft learning objectives, giving numerous examples of general and specific objectives.

Finally, we show that objectives are not all on the same level; that is, there exists a gradation between simple, concrete objectives and complex, abstract objectives.

2.1 Definitions

Generally, we can say that an objective is a kind of target. The targets of a course — the *objectives* — are what you propose that your students learn within the context of a given body of knowledge.

We'll define here the two principal types of objectives, *general* and *specific*.

General objectives. A general objective is a statement in which you express an abstract educational intention, describing the combination of lasting changes (cognitive, affective, or psychomotor) you expect in your students during the course. The statement of a general objective encompasses the statements of specific objectives that derive from it or serves as a basis for formulating them.

Specific objectives. A specific objective is a statement, as precise as possible, in which you describe, within the limits of a course topic, what students must achieve during or at the end of a learning situation or section. A specific objective permits you to link a given subject and student performance.

2.2 Principal Advantages of Formulating Objectives

Formulating objectives offers numerous pedagogical advantages, because it requires you to:

- announce your objectives clearly;

- devise teaching or learning activities that allow students to attain those objectives;
- evaluate only the activities you have announced and implemented.

The first advantage, therefore, is that *you can discuss the course clearly and precisely*, since the objectives allow you to specify not only the nature of the subjects, but also the learning you expect from your students.

The second advantage is that *you must choose only teaching methods that allow you to attain the targeted objectives*; it would, in fact, be illogical to use a method appropriate to objectives other than those specified.

Finally, the last and most important advantage is that *you must establish a direct relationship between your specific objectives and your evaluation of the students*. Thus, when you draft specific objectives, you are specifying the nature of the test questions or evaluation criteria for a given task. You can then clearly tell your students, "Here is what you should be able to do to succeed on the test," (the objectives) or "Here are the criteria I will use when I correct and evaluate your work."

As you can see, objectives are to a course what the foundation is to a building. Formulating objectives requires you to be consistent in the three principal components of your course: objectives, teaching methods, and means of evaluation. You must ensure a perfect fit among your objectives, the means you use to pursue them, and your manner of evaluating how well you and your students have attained them.

2.3 Process of Drafting Objectives

Drafting objectives is a process in which you think about the nature of what you want your students to learn within the framework of a body of given knowledge.

When we think, we generally use an approach in which we first identify general ideas, then break them down progressively into secondary ideas. When you draft the objectives of a course, you also proceed from the general to the specific, from the least precise to the most precise, keeping in mind the general objectives and the specific objectives.

In Table 2.1 (on the next page), which presents this approach schematically, you'll notice a course is a unit that corresponding to the sum of the objectives you set for your students. You first write the least precise objectives — and the most abstract; these are the *general objectives*, which describe global changes (cognitive, affective, or psychomotor) that you expect of your students.

The general objectives cover all of the *themes* that you have identified. Usually, one, two, or three statements suffice to describe these general intentions. Naturally, the number of themes varies from one course to another (Chapter 1).

Then, for each of the themes treated in the course, you draft *specific objectives,* which clarify the general objectives. They allow you to list most precisely the actions or learning associated with each course theme. The number of specific objectives associated with a theme usually varies from one to six.

2.4 Drafting General Objectives

A general objective is a short statement (one to three lines), formulated from the *professor's point of view* and beginning with a *verb.*

Table 2.1 Progressive Approach to Drafting Course Objectives

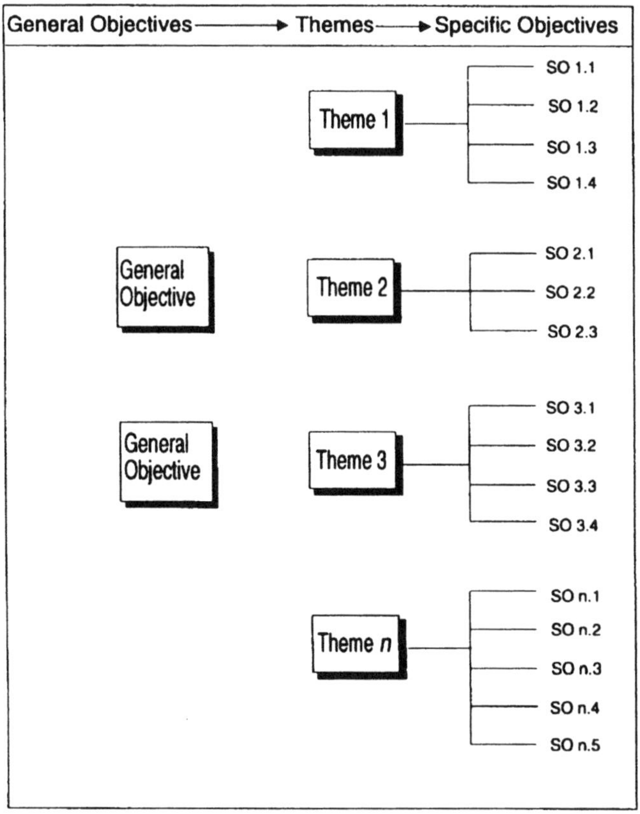

You can easily formulate the general objective(s) for a course by completing the following introductory sentence:

Course xxx aims to ...

In this sentence, we often use statements beginning with verbs or general verbal expressions, such as:

- introduce students to ...
- familiarize students with ...
- sensitize students to ...
- help students discover ...
- make students aware of ...
- make students able to ...
- develop the ability to ...
- make students appreciate the importance of ...
- supplement basic knowledge in ...

The general objectives presented in Example 2.1 are authentic, taken from engineering courses.

Example 2.1 General Objectives

The course "Computer-Aided Design" aims to:	**The course "Methodology of Engineering Projects and Communication" aims to:**
• *enable the student* to systematically design mechanical components in a CAD context; • *enable the student* to interact with mechanical analysis and CAM software.	• *give the student a theoretical and practical overview* of the work of a design engineer; • *give the student an overview* of the written and oral communication skills needed in the engineering profession.
The course "Chemical Reactor Theory" aims to:	**The course "Numerical Applications in Mechanical Engineering" aims to:**
• *help the student acquire* basic knowledge of chemical kinetics; • *explain* the design of different reactor types (batch, C.S.T.R., and tubular); • *enable the student* to choose the type of reactor appropriate to a given situation, either in terms of selectivity or in terms of conversion.	• *introduce the student* to the basic concepts of methods of finite elements and finite differences, as preparation for more specialized courses in the field; • to a lesser extent, *furnish the student* with some elementary knowledge of signal analysis and linear system frequency response.

The general objective statements presented above describe, *in terms of development*, the intentions of the course professors. That is why these objectives express the intentions only generally, in a way open to interpretation. Instructors clarify the meaning of general course objectives by drafting specific objectives.

2.5 Drafting Specific Objectives

A specific objective is also a short statement (one to three lines) beginning with an action verb, but formulated from the *student's point of view.*

To write the specific objectives, you think about what the *student must be able to do* in order to attain the general objectives, whereas to formulate the general objectives, you think about *your intention as professor.*

On average, one to six specific objectives suffice to describe what you hope a student will be able to do with regard to each of the course themes. You can draft a specific objective by completing the following introductory sentence:

> *After studying theme xxx of the course, the student should be able to ...*

This phrase is followed by a verb and one or more objects.

In Table 2.2 (on the next page), we provide a partial list of verbs frequently used in drafting specific objectives.

Notice that the verbs used in the specific objectives are more precise than those used in the general objectives. These action verbs express observable gestures, actions, and performances. Specific objectives take us beyond the intention expressed by the general objectives. Specific objectives are in fact *operational tools,* just as useful for teaching as for evaluating.

The specific objectives in Example 2.2 (on following pages) detail the general objectives presented in Example 2.1, which we repeat in order to show the relation between these two levels of objectives.

Although it is tempting to believe that specific objectives will be attained as chronologically presented, that's not the case. In fact, specific objectives can be attained in no particular order at all, and sometimes even throughout the course, rather than in a specific time frame.

The statements of the specific objectives presented in Example 2.2 are good illustrations of the progressive approach discussed earlier, in that the groups of specific objectives detail the general objectives or clarify their meaning in relation to the principal themes of the courses. Note that the specific objectives:

- refer to behavior expected from the *students;*

Table 2.2 Verbs Often Used in Drafting Specific Objectives

1	2	3
list name identify show define recognize recall	explain put into your own words interpret describe compare differentiate demonstrate	solve calculate use manipulate apply state classify modify put into practice
4	**5**	**6**
analyze organize deduce choose	design support schematize write report discuss plan	evaluate judge defend criticize justify
(The category numbers correspond to the Bloom taxonomy levels, as explained in Section 2.6 and Table 2.3.)		

- always begin with an *action verb;*
- are linked to each of the course *themes;*
- explain in detail the meaning of the *general objectives.*

Furthermore, the *average number* of specific objectives varies, from one to four in these examples, according to the different themes.

In conclusion, remember that although the process of drafting objectives moves from general to specific, the process of teaching often goes in reverse. So in a given course, you often bring your students to specific goals first; by attaining each group of specific objectives, the students can attain each of the general objectives.

2.6 Taxonomic Analysis of Cognitive Objectives

It is evident that all cognitive objectives of a course — that is, those objectives relating to knowledge — are not on the same level: some are elementary, others are based on more complex intellectual processes.

Example 2.2 Specific Objectives

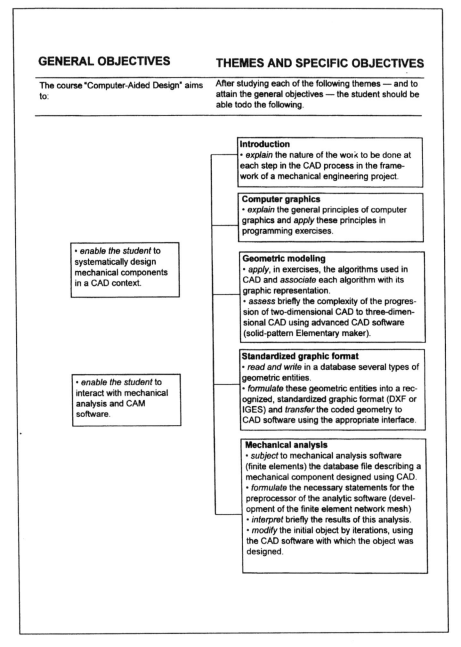

GENERAL OBJECTIVES	THEMES AND SPECIFIC OBJECTIVES
The course "Computer-Aided Design" aims to:	After studying each of the following themes — and to attain the general objectives — the student should be able todo the following.
	Introduction • *explain* the nature of the work to be done at each step in the CAD process in the framework of a mechanical engineering project.
	Computer graphics • *explain* the general principles of computer graphics and *apply* these principles in programming exercises.
• *enable the student* to systematically design mechanical components in a CAD context.	**Geometric modeling** • *apply*, in exercises, the algorithms used in CAD and *associate* each algorithm with its graphic representation. • *assess* briefly the complexity of the progression of two-dimensional CAD to three-dimensional CAD using advanced CAD software (solid-pattern Elementary maker).
• *enable the student* to interact with mechanical analysis and CAM software.	**Standardized graphic format** • *read and write* in a database several types of geometric entities. • *formulate* these geometric entities into a recognized, standardized graphic format (DXF or IGES) and *transfer* the coded geometry to CAD software using the appropriate interface.
	Mechanical analysis • *subject* to mechanical analysis software (finite elements) the database file describing a mechanical component designed using CAD. • *formulate* the necessary statements for the preprocessor of the analytic software (development of the finite element network mesh) • *interpret* briefly the results of this analysis. • *modify* the initial object by iterations, using the CAD software with which the object was designed.

Example 2.2 Continued

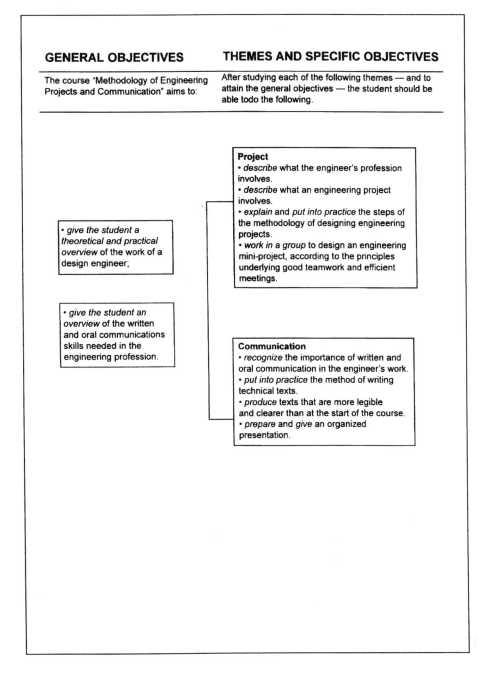

GENERAL OBJECTIVES	THEMES AND SPECIFIC OBJECTIVES
The course "Methodology of Engineering Projects and Communication" aims to:	After studying each of the following themes — and to attain the general objectives — the student should be able todo the following.
• *give the student a theoretical and practical overview* of the work of a design engineer;	**Project** • *describe* what the engineer's profession involves. • *describe* what an engineering project involves. • *explain* and *put into practice* the steps of the methodology of designing engineering projects. • *work in a group* to design an engineering mini-project, according to the principles underlying good teamwork and efficient meetings.
• *give the student an overview* of the written and oral communications skills needed in the engineering profession.	**Communication** • *recognize* the importance of written and oral communication in the engineer's work. • *put into practice* the method of writing technical texts. • *produce* texts that are more legible and clearer than at the start of the course. • *prepare* and *give* an organized presentation.

Example 2.2 Continued

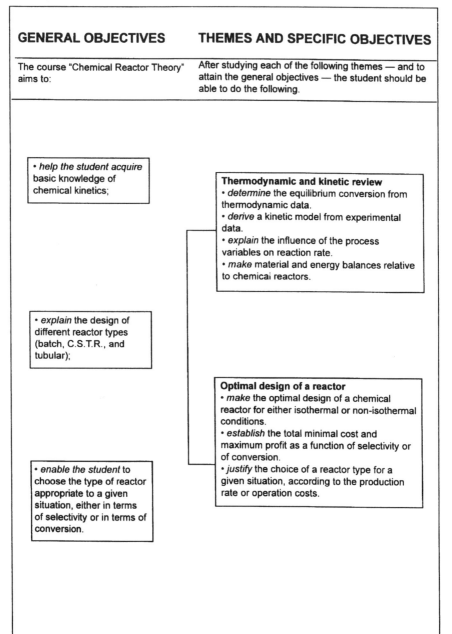

GENERAL OBJECTIVES	THEMES AND SPECIFIC OBJECTIVES
The course "Chemical Reactor Theory" aims to:	After studying each of the following themes — and to attain the general objectives — the student should be able to do the following.

• *help the student acquire* basic knowledge of chemical kinetics;

• *explain* the design of different reactor types (batch, C.S.T.R., and tubular);

• *enable the student* to choose the type of reactor appropriate to a given situation, either in terms of selectivity or in terms of conversion.

Thermodynamic and kinetic review
• *determine* the equilibrium conversion from thermodynamic data.
• *derive* a kinetic model from experimental data.
• *explain* the influence of the process variables on reaction rate.
• *make* material and energy balances relative to chemicai reactors.

Optimal design of a reactor
• *make* the optimal design of a chemical reactor for either isothermal or non-isothermal conditions.
• *establish* the total minimal cost and maximum profit as a function of selectivity or of conversion.
• *justify* the choice of a reactor type for a given situation, according to the production rate or operation costs.

Example 2.2 Continued

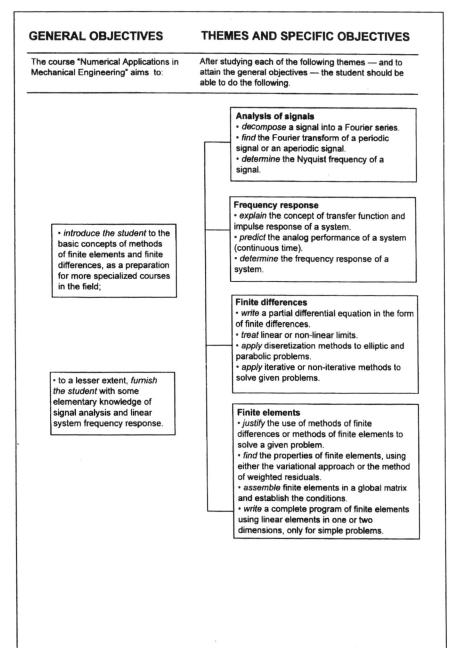

GENERAL OBJECTIVES	THEMES AND SPECIFIC OBJECTIVES
The course "Numerical Applications in Mechanical Engineering" aims to:	After studying each of the following themes — and to attain the general objectives — the student should be able to do the following.
	Analysis of signals • *decompose* a signal into a Fourier series. • *find* the Fourier transform of a periodic signal or an aperiodic signal. • *determine* the Nyquist frequency of a signal.
• *introduce the student* to the basic concepts of methods of finite elements and finite differences, as a preparation for more specialized courses in the field;	**Frequency response** • *explain* the concept of transfer function and impulse response of a system. • *predict* the analog performance of a system (continuous time). • *determine* the frequency response of a system.
	Finite differences • *write* a partial differential equation in the form of finite differences. • *treat* linear or non-linear limits. • *apply* diseretization methods to elliptic and parabolic problems. • *apply* iterative or non-iterative methods to solve given problems.
• to a lesser extent, *furnish the student* with some elementary knowledge of signal analysis and linear system frequency response.	**Finite elements** • *justify* the use of methods of finite differences or methods of finite elements to solve a given problem. • *find* the properties of finite elements, using either the variational approach or the method of weighted residuals. • *assemble* finite elements in a global matrix and establish the conditions. • *write* a complete program of finite elements using linear elements in one or two dimensions, only for simple problems.

We are going to distinguish here six levels of objectives, borrowed from the taxonomy (hierarchic classification) of cognitive domain objectives established by Benjamin Bloom (Table 2.3).

It's a good idea to compare your objectives with the Bloom taxonomy. This taxonomy is a *frame of reference* that enables you to verify the objectives pursued are really at the appropriate level. If you notice discrepancies between the level of your intentions and the taxonomic levels of the objectives you have drafted, you should correct these discrepancies to remain consistent.

In his taxonomy of cognitive domain objectives, Bloom conceives of learning knowledge as a progressive process that moves necessarily from concrete to abstract. Learning is more concrete at the elementary levels (1,2,3) and more abstract at the higher levels (4,5,6). To accomplish the learning tasks associated with a given taxonomic level, the student must first have attained the objectives of the preceding levels.

Table 2.3 Taxonomy of Learning Objectives From the Cognitive Domain by Benjamin Bloom

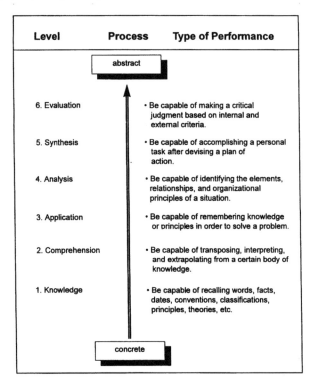

Level	Process	Type of Performance
	abstract ↑	
6. Evaluation		• Be capable of making a critical judgment based on internal and external criteria.
5. Synthesis		• Be capable of accomplishing a personal task after devising a plan of action.
4. Analysis		• Be capable of identifying the elements, relationships, and organizational principles of a situation.
3. Application		• Be capable of remembering knowledge or principles in order to solve a problem.
2. Comprehension		• Be capable of transposing, interpreting, and extrapolating from a certain body of knowledge.
1. Knowledge		• Be capable of recalling words, facts, dates, conventions, classifications, principles, theories, etc.
	concrete	

When you create a course, you choose the taxonomic levels that you judge most appropriate. However, for a college or university course, we strongly advise you to focus on the upper levels of Bloom's taxonomy of the cognitive domain.

We are now going to examine in greater detail the objectives associated with each one of the levels of Bloom's taxonomy.

2.6.1 Level 1: Knowledge

You set objectives from Level 1 — acquisition of knowledge — when you merely want your students to acquire new knowledge. To do this, you emphasize memorization of all kinds of new information: terms, definitions, facts, conventions, formulas, sequences, methods, classifications, principles, laws, etc.

Students can efficiently attain objectives limited to the simple acquisition of knowledge through almost any method of transmitting information — listening to lectures, reading texts, viewing films, observing demonstrations, listening to radio programs or conversations, etc. All of these situations are equally good ways for students to reach Level 1 objectives.

To better convey the nature of the objectives at this first taxonomic level, Example 2.3 presents some objectives taken from several courses, in no particular order.

Example 2.3 Level 1 Objectives: Knowledge

After studying theme xxx of the course, the student should be able to:

- *remember* the definitions of the three elementary principles of magnetism;
- *identify* the standard peripheral components of a computer and *list* their characteristics;
- *define* the graphic and algebraic computational methods associated with calculating the frequency response of a circuit;
- *list* the advantages and limits of manufacturing metallic components from metallurgical dust;
- *list* the areas of use relative to manufacturing metallic components from metallurgical dust;
- *name* the effects of tempering on the mechanical properties of materials and the anisotropy.
- *identify* the nature of a chemical element from its position in the periodic table;
- *list* the principal finance plans that a business firm can consider;
- *classify* the equations for partial derivatives.

All college courses include objectives from Level 1. However, you cannot set objectives from this level alone; most professors want their students to "understand." Consequently, you must select objectives from Level 2.

2.6.2 Level 2: Comprehension

You set objectives from Level 2 — comprehension — when you want your students to engage in intellectual activities beyond simple passive listening or memorization. A student who notes a piece of information does not always automatically understand it; to understand it, he or she must be able to verify the ability to transpose this information or interpret it or extrapolate from it.

A student is capable of transposing when, for example, she can formulate an explanation in her own words, answer a question, discuss a point, or verify by way of a self-test that her reasoning is logical.

A student is capable of interpreting a piece of information when, for example, he can reduce it to its essential elements, by generalizing it, comparing it with similar information, or drawing conclusions from it.

A student is capable of extrapolating when, for example, she can extract from specific knowledge implications or general consequences or identify the limits of her arguments in the context of a discussion.

Therefore, if you set objectives from Level 2, you must provide your students with pedagogical activities in which they will be able to exercise their ability to transpose, interpret, or extrapolate. You cannot merely expose your students to knowledge through lectures, because these activities only allow them to attain Level 1 objectives.

If you do not permit your students to obviously reach Level 2 cognitive behaviors (preferably before the test!), you can only hope they will understand: you do not know in fact if they really do understand. There is a discrepancy, then, between your goals and your results.

You must provide your students with pedagogical situations in which they will have to transpose, interpret, and extrapolate from information and where you will be able to verify their comprehension of the concepts presented.

You can use questions during a lecture to show whether or not students understand. Pair or team discussions can also provide evidence of understanding. Other activities that can help students attain Level 2 objectives include creating analogies, writing summaries, and explaining to a peer.

Example 2.4 (on the next page) presents a few Level 2 objectives drawn from several courses, presented in no particular order.

Example 2.4 Level 2 Objectives: Comprehension

After studying theme XXX of the course, the student should be able to:

- *explain* the nature of the work to be accomplished in each one of the steps of the CAD process within the framework of a mechanical engineering project;
- *tell in his or her own words* the steps in the methodology of designing and completing engineering projects;
- *explain* how to effect the conversion to equilibrium for a chemical reactor from thermodynamic data;
- *explain* how different radiation meters function;
- *explain* how dosimeters function in dynamic or static mode;
- *explain* why Newton's method has a quadratic convergence;
- *differentiate* among Bessel functions;
- *predict* the chemical formulas of ionic compounds formed between metals and nonmetals;
- *describe* the principal characteristics of gases and compare them with characteristics of other states of matter;
- *explain* how to determine the stress at one point of a straight girder subjected to some kind of spatial change;
- *compare* the different diagrams of pyrometallurgy of common metals.

Remember that merely setting Level 2 objectives does not mean that students will automatically attain them. When you set such objectives, you are committing to organizing activities that will allow you to verify whether your students understand (activities of transposition, interpretation, or extrapolation). You must also correct their learning if they do not properly understand. In addition, since it's no good to understand a lot of things if you cannot use them, you must set objectives from Level 3, application.

2.6.3 Level 3: Application

You can help your students attain objectives from Level 3 — application — when you put them in situations that let them verify their theoretical knowledge with simple, practical cases to solve a given problem.

Through these situations, you first make sure that your students can:

- *identify* the known and unknown elements of the problem;
- *restructure* these elements according to a known model;
- *choose* a method or principle that allows them to solve the problem;
- *solve* the problem using that method or applying that principle.

Individual exercises, homework, laboratories, and simple problem-solving in class are all activities that help students attain Level 3 objectives.

Example 2.5 presents a number of specific objectives from Level 3, again taken from several courses and simply listed one after another.

Example 2.5 Level 3 Objectives: Application

After studying theme xxx of the course, the student should be able to:

- *formulate* geometric entities in a standard graphic format (DXF or IGES) and *transfer* this geometry into a CAD program;
- *derive* a kinetic model from experimental data;
- *find* the Fourier transform of a periodic and aperiodic signal;
- *apply* discrete methods sampling to elliptic or parabolic problems;
- *write* a complete program of finite elements using linear elements in one or two dimensions;
- *use* several methods for evaluating profitability and risk for given problems;
- *calculate* the energies released or consumed in an electrochemical process;
- *solve* problems of transfer of heat and matter with convection using the analytic method and applying empirical correlations;
- *calculate* the number of theoretical steps in a separation process;
- *produce* a cabling diagram for the analog simulation of dynamic linear systems.

Here again, you must provide pedagogical activities to help your students attain the set objectives.

Attaining objectives from Levels 1, 2, and 3 implies "elementary" intellectual activities — acquiring knowledge, understanding, and solving simple problems similar to those solved in class. The next three taxonomic levels refer to more abstract intellectual activities.

2.6.4 Level 4: Analysis

You can help your students attain objectives from Level 4 — analysis — by requiring them to apply hypothetico-deductive reasoning within the framework of a given body of knowledge.

A professor who aims for objectives at this level wants each student to be able to:

- break down a given problematic situation into its constituent parts,
- identify the relationships that exist among these parts, and
- reveal the underlying principles of organization — that is, *solve* the problem.

Several activities can help students develop analytical skills: conducting personal research, doing team projects, writing monographs, defending a point of view in a seminar, completing elaborate assignments, and participating in case studies.

It is difficult to believe that students will attain Level 4 objectives in a course that does not provide such activities. Although your lectures may prove that you have sharp analytical skills, this will not lead your students to attain objectives at this level. This kind of pedagogical situation allows students to attain objectives at Level 1 or 2 at the highest because analytical skills do not develop through osmosis, by simple contact with the professor: students develop analytical skills through use. Consequently, if you have not provided your students with activities like those listed above, you cannot honestly ask them exam questions requiring an intellectual activity for which you have not prepared them. Indeed, a student cannot show spontaneously, during a test, an analytical sense more developed than he or she had upon entering the course!

In Example 2.6, we propose some specific objectives from Level 4, taken from several courses and simply listed one after another.

Example 2.6 Level 4 Objectives: Analysis

After studying theme xxx of the course, the student should be able to:

- *analyze* experimental data;
- *choose* processes of extraction or distillation adequate to obtain products of desired properties;
- *analyze* statistically experimental data coming from a laboratory;
- *solve* problems relating to assessments of heat and energy;
- *analyze* stress features to determine the mode of stress, the initial site, and the direction of the fissuration;
- *choose* an alloy for a given application and determine the processing sequence and the heat treatment required;
- *analyze* a stress break and suggest solutions to this problem;
- *analyze* simple cases of corrosion and propose remedies;
- *analyze* the financial situation of a business firm as well as its profitability and efficiency during a given period;
- *analyze* the handling needs of a factory or department;
- *analyze* pollution cases caused by engineering projects and *propose* solutions that are acceptable from the environmental point of view and from the legislative point of view in Quebec.

If you set objectives from Level 4, you must always prepare appropriate pedagogical activities. Otherwise, your objectives will remain just wishful thinking. In addition, your students will have difficulty progressing to attain objectives from Level 5, synthesis.

2.6.5 Level 5: Synthesis

You set objectives from Level 5 — synthesis — when you want to help your students develop personal expression and independence of thought in a given domain.

Synthesis, as Bloom understands it, is different from the simple summary or listing of elements; it requires more advanced intellectual activities, such as creating new elements or organizing several elements into a new, personal, and original structure that shows reflection.

You can help your students develop a sense of synthesis in several ways. One way is to have them do a personal project, in which each student communicates his or her ideas, feelings, or experiences. This project may involve any form of expression — written, oral, musical, audio-visual, computing, or any other. What's important is that each student create a structure that did not exist before, a structure that is personal, unique, and different from those of other students who take the same course and do the same assignment.

Doing assignments, preparing and making presentations, designing computer programs or audio-visual documents, and so forth are pedagogical activities likely to enable students to attain Level 5 objectives.

It is obvious that synthesis, according to Bloom, is very far from the synthesis (or summary) that the professor provides at the conclusion of a part of a course. This latter kind of synthesis does not allow students to attain Level 5 objectives; it is at the very most associated with objectives from Level 1 or 2.

A second way to encourage a student to attain Level 5 objectives is to ask him or her to devise and finalize a plan of action in keeping with the requirements of a discipline — a plan of action that you can then easily divide into several parts to have the student accomplish, alone or with other students.

Activities that require the student to devise plans of action include setting up individual or team projects, verifying hypotheses in the laboratory, solving complex problems, and preparing a course to teach to peers.

A third way to develop the students' sense of synthesis is to provide activities in which they must express, clearly and logically, their thoughts on a subject related to the course. Such activities involve abstract or intellectual activities requiring manipulation of a whole series of concepts and deducing from them a set of abstract relations, the original fruit of advanced personal reflection.

Term papers or research work are activities through which a student can prove a sense of synthesis, such as Bloom conceives it.

In brief, in order to attain Level 5 objectives, a student must be placed into situations in which he or she will be able to make the most of his or her sense of creative activity, within the framework of a given body of knowledge, to produce a set of elements organized according to an original structure — new and personal.

Example 2.7 presents a list of specific Level 5 objectives, again taken from several courses and presented in no particular order.

Example 2.7 Level 5 Objectives: Synthesis

After studying theme XXX of the course, the student should be able to:

- *develop* software to calculate processes of extraction or distillation;
- *plan* a laboratory experiment;
- *write* a laboratory report conforming to presentation norms required in geological engineering;
- *do an oral report* on the experimental work carried out by a research group;
- *write* an appraisal based on the analysis of a given stress break;
- *design* a cathodic protection system;
- *design* a series of chemical operations to separate quantitatively the elements in a solution;
- *devise* a prototype for a design competition for amphibious cars;
- *prepare* the financial report of a firm and suggest methods of evaluating stock and of depreciating fixed assets;
- *produce* a report suggesting the ergonomic improvements for a work position in order to increase productivity and comply with the laws;
- *simulate* the model of a manufacturing system in an advanced simulation language;
- *devise* a computerized management system;
- *plan* and *organize* the activities of a factory maintenance system.

For students to attain Level 5 objectives, you must organize appropriate activities, such as those presented above.

Finally, in order for their intellectual activities to approach those characterizing an expert, students must learn to exercise their critical judgment concerning their own work and that of others. To do so, they must attain the objectives of Level 6, evaluation.

2.6.6 Level 6: Evaluation

You select objectives from Level 6 — evaluation — when you encourage students to use their critical sense to evaluate ideas they have been exposed to or work they have done. For this type of evaluation, they must be able to judge an object either intrinsically — by referring to criteria of logic, coherence, or scientific precision — or comparatively — by comparing it with other similar objects. Activities of this type can truly help develop what might be called "the sense of expertise" in a given domain.

Evaluation, as Bloom understands it, constitutes an advanced activity that implies combining all the skills developed at the lower levels: knowledge, comprehension, application, analysis, and synthesis.

Discussions, seminars, debates, apologiae, written and oral critiques, and self-criticisms are several ways of helping students attain Level 6 objectives.

Students cannot acquire a critical sense simply through observation; they must exercise their critical sense through specific activities that you design and supervise. Most of the activities that permit attainment of Level 4 and 5 objectives can become activities associated with Level 6; you just need to add the "value judgment" aspect that the students must apply to their work, both in planning and after completion.

Example 2.8 shows several specific objectives from Level 6, selected in the same manner as those from the other levels.

Example 2.8 Level 6 Objectives: Evaluation

After studying theme XXX of the course, the student should be able to:

- *judge* effects that can lead to the choice of method of depreciation of fixed assets;
- *evaluate* the performance of equipment required for the auxiliary services of a factory;
- *evaluate* the environmental consequences of an engineering project on a given site.

In the framework of a course, it is not you who must attain the Level 6 objectives, but the students, through appropriate activities that you provide.

2.6.7 Taxonomies for Affective and Psychomotor Domains

In this work, we have decided to limit ourselves to the study of cognitive objectives, associated with Bloom's taxonomy of objectives. However, human learning is not limited to the acquisition of knowledge.

In fact, the act of learning also involves modification, reinforcement, or integration of several affective aspects, such as beliefs, attitudes, values, or interests.

Furthermore, in certain disciplines (medicine, nursing sciences, physical education, dental surgery, physiotherapy, etc.), learning also necessarily involves the acquisition of motor skills essential to specialized manipulations.

If your course involves learning in the affective and psychomotor domains as well as the cognitive, you must formulate objectives in each of these domains. These objectives are also classified according to different taxonomic levels. (Although the taxonomies of affective and psychomotor objectives are important, their treatment would take us beyond the scope of this work.)

If you must write affective or psychomotor objectives, you should consult the works of David R. Krathwohl for the affective domain and Anita J. Harrow for the psychomotor domain (see bibliography).

Review

Principal Advantages of Formulating Objectives

- Formulating objectives allows you to go beyond simply listing contents to describe what your students will be able to do at the end of the course.
- Formulating learning objectives consequently allows you to:
  - speak more clearly about a course — to students or to colleagues — than would the mere description of contents;
  - choose only teaching methods appropriate for helping your students attain the targeted objectives;
  - establish a direct relationship between the objectives and your evaluation of your students.
- In short, formulating objectives requires you to articulate the three principal elements of your course: the objectives, the teaching methods, and the means of evaluation.

Procedure for Writing Objectives

Three steps:

1. Draft general objectives.
2. List the themes to cover.
3. Draft specific objectives relative to each of your themes.

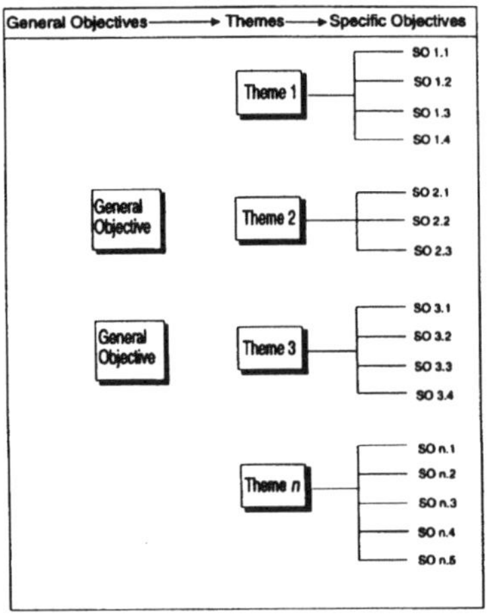

Drafting General Objectives

- A *general objective* is a statement that:
  - is short;
  - begins with a *verb;*
  - is formulated from the *professor's point of view;*
  - describes the *global changes* (cognitive, affective, or psychomotor) desired for the students.
- You formulate a general objective more easily by completing the following introductory sentence:

  Course xxx aims to ...
- In general, one, two, or three general objectives are sufficient to express the general intentions of a course.

Drafting Specific Objectives

- A *specific objective* is a statement that:
  - is short;
  - begins with an *action verb;*
  - is formulated from the *student's point of view;*
  - describes, *as precisely as possible,* the performances (cognitive, affective, or psychomotor) that the students must be able to achieve *in relation to each one of the course themes.*
- You write a specific objective by completing the following introductory sentence:

  After studying theme xxx of the course, the student should be able to ...
- The average number of specific objectives varies according to the themes, with usually one to six per theme.

Taxonomic Analysis of Objectives

- All cognitive objectives are not on the same level, as Bloom made clear in his *Taxonomy of Educational Objectives (Cognitive Domain).* This taxonomy is a frame of reference that allows you to verify whether the levels of your intentions correspond to the taxonomic levels of the objectives you have drafted. According to Bloom, there are six levels of objectives:

  1. knowledge,
  2. comprehension,

3. application,
4. analysis,
5. synthesis,
6. evaluation.

- In a college or university course, you cannot be satisfied with students attaining only cognitive objectives at the lower levels (1, 2, 3); you must focus on objectives at the higher levels (4, 5, 6).
- There are other taxonomies to help you formulate objectives from the *affective* and *psychomotor* domains.

CHAPTER 3

PLANNING TO EVALUATE LEARNING

We now approach an important aspect of course preparation: planning to evaluate your students.

We first deal with the role you intend to have evaluation play in your course: *summative* or *formative*. We define both roles and examine the pedagogical consequences of the types of evaluation that derive from them.

Next we classify the evaluation instruments into three categories (tests, assignments, and exercises). Then we suggest selection criteria for these instruments. Finally, we briefly describe the characteristics of these instruments.

To conclude, we give practical advice for designing, administering, and correcting the instruments as described.

3.1 The Role of Evaluation

Professors have different concepts of the role of evaluation. For some, evaluation serves only to verify learning at the end of the course, while for others it serves to help students improve during the course. We explore here these two points of view.

3.1.1 Evaluation for Summative Purposes

An evaluation is called "summative" when you judge learning *after* the learning has ended, assessing the knowledge acquired during the course or during part of the course.

This judgment allows you to *reach a decision* on how well a student has learned the material. You decide whether or not the student has attained the number of objectives sufficient to conclude a given stage of the course. The basis for such a decision, for example, might be a final examination or the equivalent.

Summative evaluation entails, moreover, a *definitive judgment*, which irrevocably marks the end of the learning process. Summative evaluation does not encourage the student to return to the material in order to improve his or her learning and raise the final grade.

When you do a summative evaluation, you play the role of a critic who determines whether the sum of the knowledge acquired by a student at the end of one stage of the course is enough to assign him or her at least a passing grade.

The purpose of a summative evaluation is not to help students succeed, but to grade them from the strongest to the weakest.

That is why summative evaluation often takes place within a *framework of normative reference*: it allows you to compare each student with his or her peers from the same reference group. In such a context, the best student (or the worst) becomes the norm, and all the other students in the group are compared to that student.

However, summative evaluation is not necessarily normative; it can also take place within a *framework of criterion reference*. In this case, you evaluate your students not by grading them in relation to each other, but instead against a set of success criteria. However, criterion summative evaluation still leads to a final judgment.

Criterion summative evaluation is highly recommended, even though professors often use normative summative evaluation.

Table 3.1 presents a synthesis of the principal characteristics of summative evaluation.

Table 3.1 Principal Characteristics of Summative Evaluation

Characteristics	Summative Evaluation
Time	At the conclusion of a learning activity
Goal	To make a decision
Feedback	Final judgment
Frame of reference	Sometimes normative (comparing each student against the others) Sometimes criterion (evaluating each student according to the same criteria)

Summative evaluation is necessary for all credit courses in recognized institutions. You have no choice: at the end of the course, you must provide a summative judgment — pass or fail — for each student.

On the other hand, you are free to determine the number of summative tests in a course. You can decide to require only one final test at the end of the course (written test, oral test, presentation, report, competition, etc.) or to offer several intermediary tests, before the final test, in the form of assessments, periodic or otherwise — each one usually covering several themes of the course.

Examples 3.1, 3.2, and 3.3 (on the following page) illustrate how, for three different cases, professors can use summative evaluation.

Example 3.1 Three Summative Evaluations: Two Periodic Assessments and One Final Test

In one course, the professor has planned two periodic assessments and one final test. The first assessment focuses on themes 1 to 4 and the second on themes 5 to 9; the final test covers the content of the entire course, but particularly themes 10 to 13.

The three evaluation instruments used by the professor are truly summative, because:

- each test ends a set of objectives;
- the professor does not intend, at the end of the test, to help his students review what they didn't understand;
- the professor's judgments are final.

Example 3.2 A Single Summative Evaluation: A Report and/or Presentation Related to a Project

In another course, the professor has planned to evaluate students by asking them to do a project that allows them to integrate knowledge relative to the course.

If the professor considers it sufficient to evaluate, at the end of the course, a report and/or presentation on the project, that evaluation is summative, because:

- the judgment is final and completes the project;
- students cannot go back to any part of their work to improve it to possibly raise their final grade.

Example 3.3 Summative Evaluation of Several Reports Related to Laboratory Work

In a third course, the professor asks her students to participate in several laboratory sessions in conjunction with their theoretical coursework and to write a short report on each of them.

If the professor just returns the graded reports and there are no activities to allow the students to return to what they missed, the evaluation is summative, because:

- the professor's judgment marks the end of a pedagogical activity;
- the professor's judgment, which is final, sanctions the success or failure of the students for each of the laboratory sessions.

In these three examples, the professors can judge the students' work according to a normative or a criterion reference. If normative, they will compare each student with the others and arrive at a ranking (from best to worst). If criterion, they will compare the work of each student against a series of success criteria — criteria corresponding, in the examples presented here, to test questions, a project report, or reports from laboratory work.

3.1.2 Evaluation for Formative Purposes

An evaluation is called "formative" when the professor judges learning at any moment *during* the learning process, with the goal of helping a student *better learn the current material.*

If the professor thus intervenes during the learning process, it is not to pass a final judgment on how well the students have learned the material (the evaluation would then be summative) but rather to examine their work in order to diagnose possible learning difficulties in relation to a certain number of the course objectives. If need be, the professor can furnish information or give advice to help the students *return* to that material, learn it better, and possibly improve their final grades when they take the summative test.

Formative evaluation rarely leads to results that are graded and used in calculating the final grade. Rather, it supplies students with judgments that are more *qualitative* than *quantitative.* Thus, it may, according to the situation, take the form of positive or negative comments, proposals, points to review, suggestions for rereading, or more precise pedagogical or general advice.

Each student can then return to certain aspects of his or her work and benefit from these corrections *before* the summative evaluation. Consequently, the student may be able to learn better and make greater progress toward the course objectives.

Formative evaluation is therefore very different from summative evaluation, since the goal is not to conclude a stage of the course, but rather to help the student return to the material and learn it better.

If you use formative evaluation, you are not comparing the students to each other; in this sense, formative evaluation is never normative. Formative evaluation always takes place in a framework of criterion reference: it allows you to compare the work of each student against a certain number of criteria that you have defined in advance and that specify what it means to successfully complete a given learning task.

Students are thus evaluated for themselves, not for a grade. They succeed in achieving mastery if they satisfy the criteria of success relative to that material. If not, they must return to the material.

Table 3.2 (on the next page) presents a summary of the principal characteristics of formative evaluation.

Table 3.2 Principal Characteristics of Formative Evaluation

Characteristics	Formative Evaluation
Time	During a learning activity
Goal	To improve learning
Feedback	Return to material
Frame of reference	Always criterion (evaluating all students according to the same criteria)

Examples 3.4 and 3.5 illustrate how formative evaluation can be applied in some cases.

Example 3.4 Formative Evaluation of Several Assignments

In a course, the professor has chosen to evaluate students with three assignments, corresponding to three major course themes. At the beginning of her course, she informs the students of her requirements for the content and form of the assignments, and she gives them instructions for the report to write for each assignment.

In a context of formative evaluation, the professor does not expect the report on each assignment to be completed before she corrects it. Rather, she asks the students to turn in at set dates — well before the final due date of each assignment — one or more rough drafts that show what has been accomplished. These rough drafts can present:

- an outline of the assignment;
- a timeline;
- the objectives to be attained;
- the hypotheses to be confirmed;
- a general idea of the concepts underlying the assignment;
- a table of contents;
- a summary.

The professor then comments on each of these rough drafts, according to the criteria that she has provided her students.

This evaluation is formative because:

- it takes place during the learning process, not at the end;
- it is intended to improve learning;
- it does not serve to rank the students, but rather to evaluate each student in relation to himself or herself; it helps each student progress according to the same evaluation criteria.

Example 3.5 Formative Evaluation of a Project

Let's return to the case in Example 3.2, an evaluation based primarily on a project. We saw that the professor could simply do a summative evaluation of this project. Let's see now how he could also do a formative evaluation.

Rather than evaluate only the final project report, the professor could, at certain pivotal points, ask the students to present progress reports, which he would evaluate according to criteria that he has provided.

This process is formative in that it is based on feedback and advice that he gives throughout the project. This process lets him influence the work of each student and possibly allow each student to improve the quality of the final product, which will be the only work evaluated summatively.

You can, of course, apply this iterative and qualitative procedure of formative evaluation to numerous other pedagogical formulas, such as laboratory sessions, modular teaching, learning contracts, or independent projects (Chapter 4).

3.1.3 Pedagogical Consequences for Instructor and Students

The two types of evaluation (summative and formative) can both be used in a course, even though they have different goals; they can even easily complement one another. It's up to you to decide, according to your concept of evaluation, whether or not to add formative evaluation activities to the required summative activities.

3.1.3.1 Summative Evaluation

Instructor's point of view. If you decide to evaluate your students only summatively, you must prepare and correct at least a final test — and possibly one or two periodic assessments or other tests of the same kind. For each test, you must create original questions, different every term and corresponding to the most important objectives of the course.

However, correcting a test requires you to work in seclusion for several days at a task that some professors find repetitive and unpleasant. As a result, many professors who dislike corrections choose to minimize the number of summative evaluations.

In addition, professors who choose to use summative evaluation often do so with the acknowledged goal of simplifying general planning. Indeed, in a context of exclusively summative evaluation, you can plan theoretical units independently of the tests, because the success or failure of students on an intermediary summative test has little effect on the rest of the course. After a test, you continue to present the new material, regardless of the test results.

The tests themselves are easy to administer, since every term *all* of the students take the *same tests* at the *same time* in the *same room*. Therefore, you do not have to plan different tasks or adapt to different rhythms according to the students, as you would if you were using formative evaluation. The fact that all students answer the same test questions makes correction easier, at least in theory.

Students' point of view. In general, students neither dislike nor like summative evaluations; they accept them as a necessary evil.

Indeed, the tests lead to peaks of work for them, because in general, in a course in which the professor evaluates them only summatively, they do not work each week. Rather, they concentrate their efforts on "spurts of study" or "cramming" before a summative test. These spurts generate a certain anxiety, of course, that not all students manage to effectively control.

Moreover, some students work even harder to guess what questions the professor is going to ask instead of preparing and studying intelligently with reference to the objectives. In fact, all students know that the goal of a summative test is not to show understanding of the subject matter, but to obtain the highest grade. After the test, students often forget what they have just worked so hard to learn. They receive a grade to mark their success or failure, but generally the summative test will not encourage them to reflect on the reasons for their success or failure.

As for the ideal number of summative tests per course, the students are divided. On one hand, they like courses that include several tests, because they are more reassuring: if they fail one of the tests, they can always recover on the following ones. On the other hand, they know that the more tests there are in a course, the more intensive preparation they must do. In addition, if several professors give several summative tests during the same term, the students complain about the increase in work.

3.1.3.2 Formative Evaluation

Instructor's point of view. If you also decide to use formative evaluation, you increase your workload; in fact, by definition, formative evaluation must be frequent in order to be effective, so you need to evaluate your students more often. On the other hand, purely qualitative evaluations require less time, since they do not result in grades that you have to justify. In general, then, the task of evaluation is less difficult and better distributed throughout the term. You can also see your students progress as a result of your comments, which is rewarding.

If you use formative evaluation, you may need to modify the course content several times, according to the difficulties revealed by this type of evaluation. In this sense, formative evaluation does not simplify course planning.

However, in a context of formative evaluation, teaching is likely to be less monotonous — both for your students and for you — since your courses will be different from term to term and from one group of students to the other. Indeed, your courses will seem more of an intellectual adventure than a quarterly performance of the same show.

It is difficult, although not impossible, to use formative evaluation in groups of 30 students or more. In that case, it's necessary to have assistants or work with a colleague (team teaching, Chapter 4).

Students' point of view. Formative evaluation presents several advantages for students.

- Since they are evaluated more often, they work more regularly.
- They are less anxious, given that the goal of formative evaluation is not to grade their work, but to help them improve.
- On the purely pedagogical level, each student receives considerable feedback — that is, more chances to improve than the student who receives only three grades on two periodic assessments and one final exam.
- Students who work in a context of formative evaluation eventually adopt a different attitude toward evaluation. They perceive evaluation less as a sanction and the professor less as a judge. Rather, they believe that formative evaluation will help them progress and succeed, and that the professor is more of a facilitator than a critic.

3.2 Evaluation Instruments

We will now consider the instruments you can use to evaluate your students, either summatively or as formatively.

3.2.1 Three Categories of Instruments

The number of means at your disposal for evaluating your students is relatively limited, as you'll notice in Table 3.3 (on the next page), where we have put these evaluation instruments into three categories — tests, assignments, and exercises — each with several variations.

Before describing each of these evaluation instruments in detail, we will show how a professor can choose among them.

Table 3.3 Three Categories of Evaluation Instruments and Variations

Tests	Written tests	subjective correction essay short answer objective correction multiple choice true or false matching sentence completion
	Oral tests	
Assignments	Theoretical work	thematic research informative summary critical summary bibliography literature review paper case study essay
	Practical work	project laboratory session presentation laboratory session
Exercises		training report assignment

3.2.2 Selection Criteria

When you must choose among these instruments, you cannot always make the ideal choice. In fact, you must often take into account several external factors, which then influence your way of evaluating students. The most important of these factors are:

- the taxonomic level of the objectives to evaluate;
- the number of students;
- the number of hours needed to prepare tests;
- the number of hours needed to correct tests;
- the availability of graders.

Each of these factors directly influences your judgment in choosing an instrument or combination of instruments for evaluating your students.

For example, your choice of instruments depends on the taxonomic level of your objectives. Some instruments allow you to evaluate only the attainment of objectives from Levels 1, 2, and 3 of Bloom's taxonomy of cognitive objectives. Others are appropriate for evaluating the attainment of objectives from taxonomy Levels 4, 5, and 6.

In Table 3.4, we link each of the instruments in Table 3.3 with the levels of cognitive objectives for which they are most appropriate.

Table 3.4 Correspondence Between the Evaluation Instruments and Bloom's Taxonomic Levels (Cognitive Domain)

Evaluation Instruments	Objectives Taxonomic levels					
	1	2	3	4	5	6
TESTS						
Written tests				X	X	X
composition	X	X	X			
short answer	X	X	X			
multiple choice	X	X				
true or false	X	X				
sentence completion				X	X	X
Oral tests						
ASSIGNMENTS						
Theoretical work						
thematic research				X	X	
informative summary				X	X	
critical summary				X	X	X
bibliography				X	X	X
literature review				X	X	X
paper				X	X	
case study				X	X	X
essay				X	X	X
Practical work						
project					X	X
laboratory session			X	X	X	
presentation				X	X	
training report					X	X
EXERCISES						
Homework		X	X	X		
Guided exercise		X	X	X		

1. Knowledge
2. Comprehension
3. Application
4. Analysis
5. Synthesis
6. Evaluation

As we see, written tests requiring short answers, all objective correction tests, and exercises are evaluation instruments that can be associated with objectives from the lower levels of Bloom's taxonomy (knowledge, comprehension, application).

The other instruments — essay tests, oral tests, and assignments — allow evaluation of the attainment of objectives from upper taxonomic levels (analysis, synthesis, evaluation).

Consequently, the levels of cognitive objectives you target limit your choice of evaluation instruments.

If you also take into account all of the other factors presented above (number of students, time for preparation, time for correction, availability of graders), you realize that this choice is further limited.

You must therefore make compromises that allow you to take into account both your objectives and your work conditions.

In principle, however, we think that work conditions should never prevail totally over pedagogical reasons in the choice of means of evaluation. It's hard to imagine, in fact, how you could evaluate learning without a certain logical justification.

We will now describe each of the instruments listed in Tables 3.3 and 3.4.

3.2.3 Tests

The test is a classic evaluation instrument. However, there are several variations in form, types of answers, and methods of correction.

3.2.3.1 Written Tests

The written test is the most widely known and used form of test. In this timed test, performed under supervision (except in the case of the take-home test), you ask the students to answer, in writing and in their own words, one or more questions related to the course material. You may or may not allow them to use documentation or secondary materials.

Instructors often give one or two tests during the term, which allows students to better evaluate their progress before the final test. These "assessments" are generally shorter than the final test. In addition, these mini-tests cover only one part of the material, while the final test generally requires the students to review all of the course content.

In a written test, you can use two types of questions: subjective and objective.

Subjective questions. In this type of test, you must *judge* the answers to determine how well they satisfy the criteria for correct answers. You can ask questions calling for answers that require extensive development (several lines, or even several pages) or for short answers (five lines or less).

Objective questions. In this case, the grader does not have to judge the answers but simply determine whether they are right or not. On this type of test, you can ask:

- multiple-choice questions,
- true-or-false questions,
- questions that require matching (for example, a word with a definition),
- questions requiring one-word answers or sentence completion.

Remember that questions with long answers are more appropriate for evaluating attainment of objectives from the upper levels. Questions with short answers and objective questions are better for evaluating the attainment of objectives from the first three levels.

Examples 3.6 to 3.11 illustrate the different types of questions you can ask on a written test.

Example 3.6 Long Answer

The coordinates of the vertices of the prism shown in the accompanying figure are as follows:

	x	*y*	*z*
Vertex A:	0	3	6
Vertex B:	0	10	9
Vertex C:	0	11	2
Vertex D:	7	10	9

Figure

Make the following changes:

1. Reduce the object by 50% in the directions y and *z*;
2. Double the dimension in the direction *x*;
3. Rotate the object 90° clockwise around an axis parallel to *Ox*.
   After making these changes, the vertex A of the object must be in A' (2,-4,3).
4. Establish the development necessary to obtain the total matrix of these changes. Do the development in algebraic form first, then in numerical form;
5. Calculate the coordinates of the vertices of the prism after these changes.

Example 3.7 Short Answer

By what construction method can conical helical springs be modeled if no parametric method is available?

Explain in a few lines how to arrive at this geometry.

Example 3.8 Multiple Choice

Carol works 15 hours per week for firm A, at $6 an hour; she also works 40 hours per week for firm B, at $5 an hour. She is the victim of an accident while working for firm B. Following her accident, she is totally incapable of working. What weekly gross income will serve as the base to calculate her compensation for lost income?

Write the number of the correct answer in the box.

1. $90
2. $200
3. $240
4. $275
5. $290

☐

Example 3.9 True or False

True or False

1. The specific volume of a crystalline plastic lens will diminish rapidly when, as it cools, the temperature becomes lower than transition temperature T_v.
   TRUE_____ FALSE_____
2. In general, a syndiotactic molecular structure is the one that crystallizes the best.
   TRUE_____ FALSE_____

Example 3.10 Matching

Match three of the resins below with the description that corresponds, writing its name in the appropriate blank.

Polystyrene	Epoxy
Polycarbonate	Acrylic
Vinyl	Polyester

_____ Resin used as insulation for high-tension lines; slight shrinkage from the molding; very useful with fiberglass as sheathing; the basis of a great number of structural adhesives.

_____ Resin having an excellent resistance to shock; transparent; can easily be colored.

_____ Inexpensive resin; easy to use; often used in packaging; often comes in the form of foam and is used as insulation.

Example 3.11 Sentence Completion

Put the verbs in parentheses in the appropriate or indicated tenses and moods.

1. Pour éviter toute erreur, (**vouloir**, impératif présent) _____ consulter la procédure n° 235.
2. S'il (**utiliser**) _____ le dictionnaire, il éviterait la majorité de ses fautes d'orthographe.

3.2.3.2 Oral Tests

On an oral test, you question each student individually on the course content. The structure of this type of test must not be random: the oral test must be conducted according to a precise plan that allows you to verify whether or not each student has truly attained the targeted objectives.

In an oral test, the student has little time to reflect and mentally prepare an answer. That is why a valid oral test must take at least 20 to 25 minutes, so that the student can express his or her thoughts on *several* subjects without being penalized for one or two unsatisfactory answers.

You should not use an oral test simply to measure memory or comprehension (Levels 1 and 2); it should allow you to evaluate particularly a sense of analysis, synthesis, or judgment (upper levels).

To ensure greater objectivity in conducting and evaluating an oral test, you might want to invite a colleague to serve as a jury. Unlike a written test, several factors that are difficult to control can influence the examiner's judgment during and after the oral test. For example, if you are tired and inattentive during the test, it can distort your interpretation of the students' responses.

In addition, the test process can be affected by attitudes, emotions, and feelings — whether from mutual antipathy, a sense of sexual harassment, professor intonations conveying sarcasm or irony, double messages, and so forth.

That's why we encourage you to safeguard your objectivity by appointing a colleague to help you ensure harmony during the interview and arrive at an accurate evaluation of each student. In addition, you shield yourself from possible grievances concerning your respect for personal rights and morality.

Moreover, we recommend tape recording all the interviews, for two reasons: first, in case of dispute, you can always check the recording; second, if a student contests the evaluation, the recording can serve to convince an arbitrator.

The oral test is a demanding evaluation instrument that is difficult to master. It requires you to devote a great deal of time, it causes students a lot of anxiety, and it is not always easy to evaluate. It is probably for all these reasons that they are not used very much.

3.2.4 Assignments

You can use all kinds of assignments to verify whether or not your students can attain the course objectives. There are two types: theoretical and practical.

3.2.4.1 Theoretical Assignments

Depending on the material and the objectives, theoretical work can take several general forms, all involving *writing*. Although these types of assignments may theoretically be very different, professors occasionally create hybrids (for example, thematic research accompanied by a critique or a literature review presented as an informative summary). And even though it is preferable for students to work alone on most theoretical work, some can be done in teams.

The principal theoretical types of assignments at the college and university level are:

- thematic research;
- informative or critical summary;
- bibliography;
- literature review;
- term paper;
- case study;
- essay.

Remember that theoretical assignments allow you to focus on evaluating attainment of objectives from the upper levels of Bloom's taxonomy.

Thematic research. The goal of a thematic research project is for the student to increase his or her knowledge on a specific course subject, without being obliged to cover the subject exhaustively. In fact, it's often the student who determines the breadth and depth of the project, according to his or her interests and the time available.

Although a report on thematic research can vary greatly in length from one teaching situation to another, it's generally about 10 pages.

To do thematic research properly, the student must:

- review documentation in several works related to the chosen topic;

- spend several hours reading these works to collect, analyze, and organize the important information;
- construct an outline of the report, which should give an account of the knowledge acquired from the readings;
- write the report.

In general, when assigning thematic research, you should not require the student to take a stand or critique the information and ideas drawn from the reading.

Summary. A summary of a book or articles, like a thematic research project, allows the student to learn more about a given subject, except that for the summary, he or she concentrates on a single work (often imposed) or on one or more journal or periodical articles.

The professor can assign two types of summaries, either *informative* or *critical*:

Informative summary. In an informative summary, the student simply gives a concise but complete account of his or her readings. This type of summary does not require any criticism or evaluation of the readings. An informative summary is in a way a documented report devoted to a single book or to one or more articles.

Critical summary. In a critical summary, the student first does an informative summary, then gives a critique (internal or external) of what he or she has read.

The *internal* critique allows the student to deal with the formal elements of the work: the logic, coherence, argumentation, precision, etc. The *external* critique permits him or her, using data from outside the work, to discuss the strengths and weaknesses of the author's ideas. It goes without saying that the critical summary targets essentially upper-level objectives.

The summary should be shorter than the work it summarizes, generally between three and five pages, depending on the size of the work.

Bibliography. A bibliography is a project done in a library. It consists of making a list of a fairly extensive number of works on a given subject.

The subject is assigned by the professor or chosen by the student. These days, bibliographies are usually compiled using computerized data bases of bibliographical references classified by subject. The bibliography allows the student to attain upper-level objectives.

To perform such a search, the student must define the subject very precisely. He or she must first find the key words that clearly delimit the subject, then identify a certain number of variables — bibliographical or personal (according to the interests of the researcher) — in order to limit the search and eliminate hundreds of unnecessary references. After obtaining the desired references, the student must use summaries of the works to determine which are appropriate. The final product then takes the form of a list of references classified by categories.

The length of the bibliography varies greatly, depending on the number of references selected. It's not useful to list too many references; in fact, that's an indication that the research was probably poorly defined and that the list includes references that are not directly appropriate.

Literature review. Literature review is a step subsequent to the bibliography: the student reads all of the listed texts and gives an account of his or her reading in the same manner as for an informative summary or a thematic research project.

The literature review, however, is a work of greater breadth than the thematic research or the informative summary — if only for the number of works to consult, the synthesis to complete, and the length of the review (25 to 50 pages). The literature review also permits a student to attain upper-level objectives.

Term Paper. In a term paper, the student must report his or her thoughts on an assigned subject. The term paper is primarily characterized by the rigor and logic of the arguments: the student's thoughts must be neither gratuitous nor freely presented .

The thought and argumentation must always be based on facts, proof, and logical reasoning. The paper has a classic construction — introduction, development, conclusion — and rarely exceeds 10 to 15 pages. By its structure and the rigor of thought that it imposes, the paper targets the attainment of upper-level objectives.

Case study. In a case study, the student must analyze a concrete problematic situation related to one of the subjects studied in a course.

The case — presented by the professor in a written document of one or two pages — is often a real situation described using authentic information. It always leads to an emergency or a crisis that requires the student to make a diagnosis and a decision, referring to the knowledge he or she has acquired in the course.

In two to five pages, each student analyzes the problematic situation and applies his or her knowledge (theoretical or abstract) to find a solution leading to a concrete action. In general, you should use each student's work in class, either in group discussions or when you work with the entire class. The case study also aims at objectives from the upper levels of Bloom's taxonomy.

Essay. The essay differs from the theoretical work presented thus far in the freedom of expression that characterizes it.

In an essay, the student must present a personal and original vision of a given subject. In order to do this, he or she chooses a central perspective and uses it to develop his or her thought on the subject. Aside from the fact that an essay must include an introduction, development, and conclusion, the student is free to choose a point of view and develop the essay as he or she thinks best. The essay may take any of the literary forms — dialogue, apologia, letter, etc. — and any of the tones — personal, humorous, sarcastic, etc. The length of an essay can vary greatly, although it should take no more than 10 to 15 pages. The essay favors the attainment of objectives from the upper levels of Bloom's taxonomy.

3.2.4.2 Practical Assignments

Having described assignments based on theoretical research, we will now present assignments of a practical nature: projects, laboratory sessions, presentations, and training reports.

Project. A project is a work generally performed by a team of students who meet regularly and progress by steps to find a solution to a given problem. To complete a project, the members of the team must:

- identify the nature of the problem;
- select objectives, establish a timeline, and divide the responsibilities and tasks;
- devise several solutions to allow attainment of the determined objectives;
- select a single solution;
- choose the means of solving the problem.

Students can do projects in the most diverse areas, such as architecture, engineering, social science, computer science, art, or audio-visual studies. Depending on the field, however, the final product can vary greatly: blueprints, social action with a given group, a computer program or video document, a prototype, a report, a presentation, an artistic activity, or a recording.

The project may be either real or simulated.

Real project. In this case, students are placed in a real work situation. That is, they must do a project for a real client. This type of project requires close collaboration between your institution and a business. The project faces all the constraints of "real life": time, money, and resources.

Simulated projects. In this case, you take a real situation and deliberately eliminate the constraints that are not absolutely necessary to the course objectives: you can free students from budgetary responsibilities or remove certain steps that are not useful in an instructional context.

A project permits evaluation of the attainment of objectives from the upper levels of Bloom's taxonomy.

Laboratory session. A laboratory session consists of a practical project that you assign to a team in order to evaluate the attainment of some of the course objectives. Professors often give students a written document presenting the objectives and explaining the experiments to carry out and the nature of the report to produce.

Some laboratory work, the "recipe book" type, demands little creative intelligence and initiative from the students, who must simply apply the written instructions in the laboratory notebook. These projects allow evaluation of the attainment of Level 3 objectives (application).

Other laboratory projects, pedagogically more interesting, require students to design an experimental procedure to verify certain hypotheses. They allow students to show that they have attained objectives from Levels 4 and 5 (analysis and synthesis). In all cases, the students must produce a written report of several pages or less.

Presentation. The presentation that one or more students make to the class at the conclusion of a practical project usually is based on a text written by the student(s). This type of presentation, generally short (15-20 minutes) often includes a period for questions.

The two principal objectives are:

- to allow all of the students in the class to profit from the work of one or more of their peers;
- to allow each student to develop oral communication skills needed by all professionals.

This type of presentation allows the professor to evaluate attainment of Level 5 objectives.

Training report. A training report is a practical project assigned to a student who has completed training in a work environment.

The goal of a training period is to provide the student the opportunity to show that he or she has acquired the professional knowledge and competence necessary in his or her future profession.

In a training period, a student must confront numerous real situations, analyze problems, and plan a strategy to solve them. *A posteriori,* the student must also judge the quality or effectiveness of his or her professional work, typically using two documents:

- the journal, in which the student records his or her remarks and comments;
- the training report, which the student writes at the end of the training period to summarize the events of the training and evaluate his or her perception of strengths and weaknesses on the professional level.

Generally, two supervisors oversee the progress of a student in training: a professor and a professional from the work environment that the student is entering. Their task is to advise the student and observe and evaluate his or her real or simulated professional acts.

Needless to say, a training period allows the professor to evaluate attainment of cognitive objectives from all levels — especially from the upper levels — as well as affective and psychomotor objectives.

3.2.5 Exercises

We now present the last category of ways to evaluate attainment of certain objectives: exercises. Here we discuss the assignment and the guided exercise in particular.

Assignment. An assignment is work that a student must do "at home," most often weekly, and that allows progressive evaluation of his or her learning.

The nature, form, and length of assignments can vary considerably from one course to another. However, in all cases, the assignments involve a direct application of knowledge freshly acquired in class, in that they allow students to verify whether they have understood the presented material. The length of time required for the assignments must not exceed several hours.

When correcting an assignment, you can either focus on the accuracy of the answers or — more interesting pedagogically — focus primarily on the intellectual route taken by the student to solve a problem and secondarily on the accuracy of the answers.

Some professors require students to do their assignments using the methodical procedure of problem-solving that they propose as a model.

The objectives targeted in assignments are from Levels 2 and 3.

Guided exercise. A guided exercise is an exercise done in class, with the professor present. There are two types of guided exercises: one done by the professor, the other done by the students.

In the first case, the professor solves the stated problem, on the board or otherwise, in front of the students, who can ask questions, of course. With this type of guided exercise, students learn by imitating the professor.

In the second case, the students solve the problem, working alone or in small groups. The professor is there to help the groups in difficulty as needed or to give short, general clarifications when the majority of the students are stopped by the same difficulty. This type of guided exercise allows the students greater intellectual activity.

Here again, some professors require students to solve the problems according to a specific methodic procedure. Guided exercises allow professors to verify attainment of objectives from Levels 2, 3, and 4 (comprehension, application, and analysis).

3.3 Practical Advice

We now offer some practical advice for each of the operations summarized in Figure 3.1 — first for the tests, then for the assignments and exercises.

3.3.1 Tests

3.3.1.1 Developing the Test

If you choose to evaluate your students with tests, you must write an original test for each evaluation. To do this, you must:

- determine the content of each test;
- recall the objectives set for the material to be tested;
- recall the taxonomic level of these objectives, so that you ask only questions in line with your original intentions;
- bear in mind the length of time anticipated for the test, or establish it;
- determine the type and number of questions to ask, in accordance with the anticipated length of time;
- provide for several equivalent forms of the same test, to avoid copying, in the following cases:
    - in large classes, if the seats are very close (for example, test A for the even rows, test B for the odd rows);
    - if students cannot all be present for the test at the scheduled time (for example, test A for the scheduled period, test B for the second period);

Figure 3.1 Steps in Preparing and Administering an Evaluation Instrument

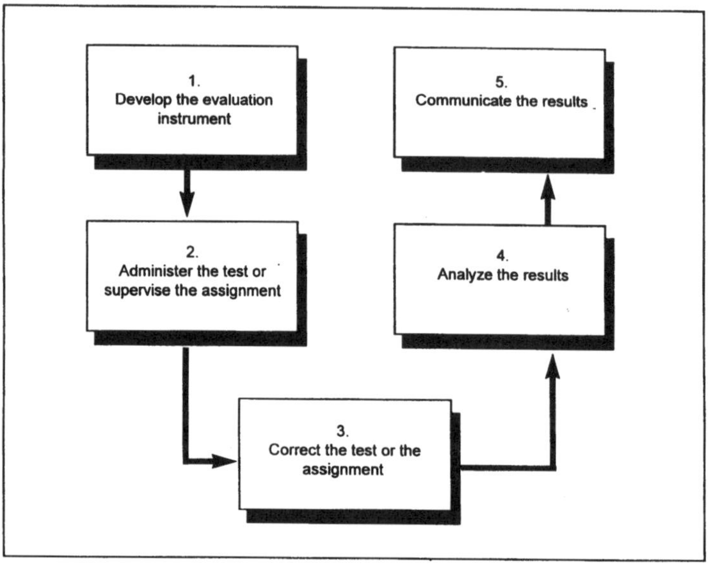

- if two groups of students will be taking the same test at different times (for example, test A for the first group, test B for the second group);

- provide for several monitors for very large groups or for when two groups take the same test at the same time in two rooms;
- plan for graders, if you will have any, and train them so that they correct the test uniformly.

Once you have completed the preliminary steps, you can:

- write the test questions;
- write the correction criteria for each question;
  - For subjective corrections, write out each answer completely or draw up the list of essential components it must include. Also, plan the grading scale and give examples of typical errors. The grader will thus be able to compare the students' answers against the correction criteria and the corresponding scale.
  - For objective corrections, prepare a list of correct answers.
- write the necessary information and instructions for the student copy of the test;

- number and title of the course,
- your name,
- length of the test,
- name and any other student identification,
- types of expected answers (essay, short answer, multiple choice, etc.),
- weight assigned to each question,
- type of documentation or materials students may use,
- consequences of copying or cheating.

Finally, after writing the test, you should ask a colleague or collaborator what he or she thinks of the final product. In this way, you can generally benefit from constructive comments concerning:

- the fit between your questions and objectives,
- the degree of difficulty of the test relative to the average level of the students,
- the length of the test,
- the clarity of the questions and instructions.

3.3.1.2 Administering the Test

When you administer the test, you must verbally give clear instructions on taking the test. You must:

- write on the board, before the students arrive, the number and name of the course, your name, the start and finish times;
- require that all students settle down and remain quiet;
- read aloud the instructions that appear on the student copy;
- answer any student questions;
- distribute the test copies and bluebooks, if any.

You must also make sure that the test takes place in conditions identical for all — that is, that there is no copying or cheating.

Although it's unpleasant to admit it, cheating is unfortunately a reality. Consequently, we advise the following:

- As you read the instructions, explain to the students, clearly and firmly, what behaviors might suggest copying or cheating, as well as the penalties. Usually, this single explicit precaution discourages potential cheaters;

- Actively watch the students during the entire test period;
- Avoid reading anything or attending to any business whatever that might implicitly encourage cheating;
- If you have more than one monitor, synchronize their movements, in order to watch simultaneously the front and the back of the room. Do not answer individual questions from several students at the same time, leaving the group without surveillance.

Finally, to help students better allocate their time on the different parts of the test, every 15 or 30 minutes you should indicate on the board the number of minutes remaining.

When the test is over, you should collect the copies yourself, in order to systematically check each copy.

3.3.1.3 Correcting the Test

To ensure all students the same chances of success, you must correct the tests systematically and impartially.

That's why we discourage using normative corrections, in which you assign grades by comparing students' tests to differentiate among the poor, the average, and the good.

Rather, we recommend comparing each test against evaluation criteria written out in advance — criteria that describe in detail what constitutes correct answers. Moreover, we recommend establishing a grading scale that allows you to calculate the total grade according to the weight assigned to each question.

When the rules are clearly specified, test correction causes fewer problems.

However, when there are several graders, you should start by correcting several tests with them. That way you can solve any problems of understanding or interpreting the grading scale and reduce the chance that tests will need to be corrected a second time.

You are ultimately responsible for your graders' work. You must therefore prepare them for their task and ask them, afterward, if they have identified any problem cases. You will thus be able to better explain to students why they lost points, for example. A few minutes spent preparing and reviewing the corrections will avoid many problems.

There are at least two ways to correct a test that seem to produce comparable results — *horizontal* and *vertical*.

With *horizontal* correction, you first correct question 1 for all of the students, then question 2, and so on, which allows you to concentrate on one single question at a time. On the other hand, this way of doing it accentuates the repetitive character of correcting, since you may spend several hours correcting the same question.

With *vertical* correction, you correct each student's copy from the first to the last question.

Ideally, you should annotate the tests as you correct. When students receive their corrected tests, they try to understand where they made mistakes: if there are no comments on their tests, they are not any better off than if they had not received their tests.

So we encourage you to annotate the test, even though it requires a lot of time. In addition, we recommend that you annotate and comment directly on the tests, rather than on a separate sheet of paper. The students will understand their mistakes better if the comments appear next to their answers. In addition, in case a student questions a grade, he or she will be less tempted to contest the validity of your comments — or even deny that you made any.

3.3.1.4 Analyzing the Results

After correcting the test, you can identify the questions the students answered successfully, then analyze the results to try to identify the causes of failure:

- poor preparation by students,
- inadequate teaching,
- poorly formulated questions,
- point distribution or grading scale that doesn't do justice to the students' efforts,
- an overly difficult test,
- too little time.

There are many aspects you must explore before continuing your teaching, because the new materials will build on the material tested.

If the problems are due to something you did wrong (a poorly formulated question, for example), you must change the weight assigned to that question in the overall grade of the test or simply eliminate it. Then, through the rest of the course, the students will maintain confidence in your ability to evaluate them fairly.

3.3.1.5 Communicating the Results

It's important to return the corrected tests to the students as soon as possible — so that they can become aware of any learning problems and correct them quickly.

However, it's not always possible to do so with large classes, when tests may take several weeks to correct and return. To reduce the inconveniences of such a delay, you can post a corrected copy of the test immediately afterward. In the case of essay or short-answer items, you would note the necessary elements that you expected students to provide for each item.

You can even give a copy of this corrected test to each student, which will allow you to discuss the test with students in the next class period, to solve any questions that your students still might not understand, and to answer their questions.

Later, when you return the test results to your students, you can briefly answer any particular questions.

3.3.2 Assignments and Exercises

In this section we provide some *general* practical advice on preparing and correcting assignments and exercises. We do not offer specific advice for each type of assignment or exercise; you can easily adapt this general advice to the type of assignment or exercise you have in mind for evaluating your students.

3.3.2.1 Developing the Evaluation Instrument

The principal complaint that students make to professors who give them assignments or exercises is the lack of clarity or precision concerning the *nature* of the work to be done and the *form* of the final product.

We thus suggest that you always provide students with written instructions, not verbal — "words fly away, but writing will stay." Instructions must describe clearly and concisely the nature and form of the work to be done.

In order to do this, you must first:

- identify the objectives you want your students to attain through this assignment or exercise;
- determine whether the taxonomic levels of the objectives truly correspond to what you want your students to achieve;
- evaluate the time required for the work to determine whether the scope of the work is adequate.

After that, you can write your instructions and distribute them to the students. Depending on the nature of the assignment, this document might include any of the following elements:

- number and title of the course,

- your name,
- description of the nature of the assignment,
- objectives,
- procedural steps for the assignment,
- evaluation criteria and relative weights of these criteria,
- time frame, with intermediate dates and final due date for the assignment,
- instructions on the form, length, or items to include in the table of contents (final report),
- list of materials, facilities, etc. at the students' disposal,
- your requirements for the distribution of the assignment activities (group work),
- list of times when the students can meet with you,
- specific requirements (final presentation, for example).

3.3.2.2 Supervising Assignments

If you choose to use assignments to evaluate your students, you must not simply give instructions at the beginning of the session and then read the final product. You must play a very active role with the students as they work through the assignment.

We even believe that your formative evaluations as the work progresses are more important pedagogically than your summative evaluation of the work. In fact, if you use formative evaluation, you improve the quality of the students' work, promote better learning, and ultimately help them earn better grades.

To supervise, you can divide the assignment into *well-defined* steps, for example, and require short reports of the steps — reports that the students can submit to you or present in class. Whatever you decide to do, however, it must not take too much time and must provide students with comments, criticism, and encouragement on their work.

In addition, as you supervise, you must constantly remind the students of the objectives of the assignment, so that they do not become too preoccupied by the details of their work and lose sight of the goals. This perspective that you promote helps the students focus on the quality of their learning experience, which otherwise might be superficial and transient.

3.3.2.3 Correcting Assignments

In correcting an assignment or exercise, you must be as systematic and impartial as for a test.

Thus, we advise against using normative corrections and recommend using weighted evaluation criteria and a grading scale. It's a good idea, however, to reserve one part of the weighting for an overall criterion that allows you to evaluate the whole of the work. Here again, it's appropriate to write comments; the advice given above for comments on tests applies as well to comments on assignments.

3.3.2.4 Analyzing the Results

After correcting the assignments, you must assess what the students have accomplished. You must ask yourself the following questions:

- To what extent have they attained the set objectives?
- Was the scope of the assignment adequate?
- Did any steps block progress on the assignment?
- Was the group work profitable?
- Were assignments presented in the required form?
- Did the formative evaluations give the expected results?

The answers to all of these questions will help you improve your instructions for future assignments.

3.3.2.5 Communicating the Results

You can generally return corrected assignments in class, although some may take weeks to correct. If you are unable to return assignments before the end of the term, you must establish a procedure for returning them and communicating the results:

- Notify the students of the date they will be able to pick up their corrected work.
- Write the overall grade very conspicuously at the top of the first page.
- Provide below the overall grade the breakdown of grades for each criterion, so students can easily identify where they lost points. If need be, discuss the reasons.
- Provide below the breakdown brief comments for each of the partial grades.
- Annotate briefly, if possible, the text of the assignment.

In spite of the many inconveniences of correcting assignments or exercises, and although it's tiresome and repetitive, we strongly encourage you to take your teaching seriously by offering students a quality perspective on the work they have accomplished.

Review

Role of Evaluation

Characteristics of summative and formative evaluation

Characteristics	Summative Evaluation	Formative Evaluation
Time	At the conclusion of a learning activity	During a learning activity
Goal	To make a decision	To improve learning
Feedback	Final judgment	Return to material
Frame of reference	Sometimes normative (comparing each student with the others)	Always criterion (evaluating all students according to the same criteria)

Summative evaluation is not really your choice, since it's necessarily a part of all education for credit.

On the other hand, adding formative evaluation to summative evaluation is a *decision* for you alone to make. It's a decision that influences the choice and frequency of evaluation, as well as the choice of teaching methods (Chapter 4) and the syllabus of activities for the entire course (Chapter 6).

Evaluation Instruments

Criteria for selecting an evaluation instrument:

- Level of objectives to evaluate,
- Number of students,
- Length of time to prepare the test,
- Length of time to correct the test,
- Availability of graders.

Categories of evaluation instruments

Tests	Work	Exercises
Written tests Oral tests	Theoretical work Practical work	Assignments Guided exercises

Practical Advice

1. Developing the evaluation instrument
   - Determine the course content to be evaluated.
   - Verify the level of objectives targeted and the relevance of the means chosen to evaluate achievement.
   - Verify the level of difficulty and the length of the test.
   - Write the evaluation criteria.
   - Write the general instructions for taking the test or doing the exercise or assignment.
   - Ask a colleague for advice on the final product.
2. Administering the test or supervising the assignment
   - Try to eliminate all possibility of copying or cheating by clearly explaining what constitutes copying and cheating and by reminding your students of the established penalties.
   - In the case of assignments, break them down into steps and require reports on those steps so that you can evaluate progress.
3. Correcting the test or assignment
   - Correct systematically and impartially. Avoid comparing students.
   - Compare each test or assignment against the evaluation criteria given to the students.
   - Use a grading scale.
   - Write your comments and annotations directly on the test or assignment.
   - If you have graders, train them and supervise their work: you alone are responsible for correcting and grading.
4. Analyzing the results
   - Assess the successes and failures and try to determine the cause of failures.
5. Communicating the results
   - Return tests to the students as soon as possible.
   - If a delay is unavoidable, distribute a corrected copy to the students and discuss it in class as soon as possible.
   - In the case of an assignment or an exercise, write down on the first page the overall grade, the grades given for each criterion, and brief comments on these partial grades.

CHAPTER 4

CHOOSING YOUR TEACHING METHODS

The growth in the number of teaching methods is a recent phenomenon, the result of the rapid development of knowledge in educational psychology since the early 20th century. Each new method is a field application of work in educational psychology or learning psychology.

At the beginning of the century (1900-1930), in reaction to the artificial aspect of learning "by heart" inherited from the 19th century, new forms of education appeared *active methods* and *methods centered on problem-solving*. The latter led to such teaching methods as learning projects, work environment training, seminars, peer learning, and case studies.

A little later (1930-1960), we witnessed the birth of *individualized teaching methods*, stemming from the behaviorist theory of learning and intended to favor the learning of each student at his or her own pace and according to his or her abilities. Individualized methods include programmed learning, modular learning, audio-tutorial learning, teaching through individual instruction (Section 4.2.3.2), and personalized education.

More recently (1960-1980), developments in cognitive psychology — which says the student must process information in order to learn — led to *teaching formulas* that are centered primarily on the student and his or her in-depth treatment of the information, as opposed to methods centered on the professor who treats the information for the students. Learning through problem-solving — also known as problem-based learning — is a good example of this teaching method.

To help you deal with the problem of choosing activities (whether in class or at home) to help students attain the course objectives, we use this chapter to classify teaching methods into three categories. Then we attempt to determine whether one of these methods is superior to the others, and we analyze the criteria that should help you choose the "right" teaching method or combination of methods. Finally, we describe in greater detail each teaching method.

4.1 Various Teaching Methods

Before presenting teaching methods (Table 4.1), it seems useful to distinguish between two concepts that many professors still confuse: teaching methods and teaching materials.

A *teaching method* is a particular way to organize pedagogical activities that are consciously implemented according to certain rules — sometimes by the professor, sometimes by the student. The goal is to help students attain the given objectives as effectively as possible.

Teaching materials, on the other hand, are the technical objects used by the professor or students within the framework of a teaching method: audio-visual aids, computers, written documents, etc.

Therefore, a professor cannot have audio-visual teaching *methods* or computer science teaching *methods*.

4.1.1 Three Categories of Teaching Methods

The number of teaching methods is limited; we have listed about 30 at most, including variations (Table 4.1). These teaching methods can be grouped into three categories:

- methods based on *different forms of lectures;*
- methods favoring *discussion* or *group work;*
- methods based on *individual learning.*

In Section 4.2, we will describe in greater detail each of the teaching methods listed in Table 4.1 (on the next page).

4.1.2 The "Best" Teaching Method

You might wonder whether one of these methods is better than the others. The answer is no; research on teaching methods, has not been able to prove the supremacy of any particular method.

Rather, it seems that the effectiveness of a teaching method is circumstantial, depending on the combination of the following factors:

- the nature of the students in the class;
- the subject matter;
- the professor's personality;
- the physical and material conditions;
- the targeted objectives.

Nature of the Students in the Class. Not all students benefit from a teaching method in the same manner. Those who exhibit learning difficulties obtain better results with structured methods, in which the work is prepared by the professor. On the other hand, those whose intellectual potential is "normal" or superior benefit more from less-structured methods that allow them more initiative. We must avoid extremes, however. Research on the effectiveness of teaching methods has shown that a total lack of structure is as ineffective as too much structure.

You cannot choose a teaching method simply because it's easy for you or because it just feels right. If you want to optimize learning, you must

Table 4.1 The Three Categories of Teaching Methods

Presentation	Formal presentations	Lecture by a single professor Series of lectures by several professors
	Informal presentations	Informal presentation by the professor Demonstration Presentation of a case Presentation by students
Discussion or Group Work	Seminars	Classic seminar Nisbet propositions Debate
	Case studies	Harvard method Dramatized case Simplified case Pigors technique Case writing by students
	Peer teaching	Project learning through problem-solving Directed work or workshop Learning unit Simulation Educational game Role play
	Others	Laboratory session Micro-teaching Team teaching
Individual Learning	Guided work	Learning contract Reading program Training period Cooperative teaching Distance teaching

Table 4.1 Continued

Individual Learning (con't.)	Individual work	Modular teaching Audio-tutoring Individually prescribed instruction Personalized system of instruction Programmed teaching

choose teaching methods that correspond to the characteristics of the students in your class.

Subject Matter. The material also directly influences the choice of teaching methods. Subject matter that is more theoretical than practical lends itself very well to lectures, discussions, or readings. On the other hand, practical subject matter of a practical nature is better suited to methods favoring application, such as projects, problem-solving, peer teaching, simulations, and laboratory sessions.

Instructor's Personality. The personal and professional qualities of the professor also constitute a significant factor in choosing a teaching method. Those who are poor at public speaking might find it difficult to give presentations; others cannot provide an individual consultation without feeling tempted to lecture. Some feel at ease when they lead groups; others succeed in guiding students only by controlling all of their actions. Indeed, all of the theoretical virtues of a teaching method are worthless if the method doesn't fit the professor's personality.

Physical and Material Conditions. The circumstances of a course may support or undermine the use of certain teaching methods. For example, a professor can use discussion methods only with smaller classes. In order for group work to be effective, the professor needs assistants to give students more opportunities for consultation. If a laboratory is inadequately equipped, the professor must form too many groups, which often makes them less effective.

Targeted Objectives. There is no one teaching method that helps students attain all types of objectives. Some are more suitable for simple, concrete objectives, while others are better for more complex, abstract objectives. Some are appropriate for affective and psychomotor objectives; others are definitely not.

Although there is no best teaching method, research has led to the following general conclusions:

- All teaching methods are equivalent when it's a question of attaining simple objectives, such as knowledge and comprehension (Levels 1 and 2 of Bloom's taxonomy).
- Teaching methods that are more "student-centered" are especially good for objectives associated with long-term memorization, development of thinking (upper levels of Bloom's taxonomy), development of motivation (upper levels of the taxonomies of affective objectives), and learning transfer.
- The superior results obtained with certain teaching methods are apparently less attributable to the methods themselves than to the quantity and quality of personal intellectual work that they encourage.

We repeat, there is no best teaching method. However, teaching methods that are more "student-centered" seem more formative, more conducive to significant learning, and more likely to increase memorization and learning transfer than "professor-centered" methods.

4.1.3 Selection Criteria

To help you more easily choose a teaching method or combination of methods, we have designed a matrix (Table 4.2) comparing the families of methods identified in Table 4.1 with five criteria likely to influence your choice:

- the levels of cognitive objectives targeted;
- the degree to which a method promotes independent and continuous learning;
- the degree of control exercised by the student;
- the number of students a method can accommodate;
- the number of hours of preparation, student contact, and correction that a method requires.

Levels of Cognitive Objectives Targeted. When we speak of levels of objectives, we mean the three lower levels of Bloom's taxonomy of cognitive objectives (knowledge, comprehension, and application) on the one hand, and the three higher levels of the same taxonomy (analysis, synthesis, and evaluation) on the other. To identify the methods that help students attain objectives from one or the other of these two levels, we use the codes LL and HL.

Degree to Which a Method Promotes Independent and Continuous Learning. The issue here is the potential of a method to encourage students to acquire and develop certain work skills: planning a learning task and verifying its accomplishment, classifying information and identifying major points, organizing time and distributing efforts, controlling the quality of personal work, organizing group work, developing motivation to learn, and so on. To indicate the degree to which a method promotes independent and continuous learning, we mark them as Low, Medium, and High.

Degree of Control Exercised by the Student. How much a student controls his or her learning considerably influences the quality of that learning. Thus, the fact that a student must (or can) plan his or her learning makes that student more responsible; because of this responsibility, which generates a deeper motivation, learning is more meaningful, lasts longer, and transfers more easily.

A student can also exercise control over the nature of the objectives, the degree of content depth, the manner of assimilating this content, and even the methods of evaluating attainment of the objectives.

To classify the teaching methods according to degree of student control, we indicate Low, Medium, and High.

Number of Students a Method Can Accommodate. The number of students a teaching method can accommodate varies. The more students, the fewer possibilities for interactions, assessments, individual supervision, or feedback between the professor and students, and feedback among the students.

The number of students can be Low (from 1 to 15), Medium (15 to 30), High (30 to 60), or Very High (more than 60).

Number of Hours of Preparation, Student Contact, and Correction That a Method Requires. Different teaching methods require a different number of hours of preparation, student contact, and correction.

To classify the teaching methods according to the criterion of time, we indicate Low, Medium, High.

As the data in Table 4.2 (on the next page) show, teaching methods based on lectures are centered on the professor, who transmits information to the students; for this reason, these methods target only lower-level objectives. They do very little to encourage independent and continuous learning, because the professor controls the activities. However, the professor who lectures can accommodate very large groups: the number of students may be limited only by the range of the professor's voice.

Finally, the professor spends only a medium amount of time on the lecture.

All other teaching methods — those that favor discussion or group work as well as those based on individual learning — permit students to attain

Table 4.2 Criteria for Selecting Teaching Methods

Teaching Methods / Selection Criteria	Presentations		Discussions or group work			Individual learning	
	Formal	Informal	Seminar	Case study	Peer teaching	Guided work	Individual work
Levels of cognitive objectives	LL	LL	UL	UL	UL	UL	UL
Degree of promoting independent and continuous learning	Low	Low	Medium	Medium	High	High	High
Degree of control exercised by the student	Low	Low	Medium	High	High	High	High
Number of students accommodated	High	High	Medium	Medium	Medium	Low	High
Number of hours of preparation, contact, and correction	Medium	Medium	Low	Medium	High	High	High

upper-level objectives. They also favor more or less independent and continuous learning, and they give students a greater degree of control over their learning. However, by and large, these methods can accommodate only groups of medium size. One exception is a method based on individual learning, which — once set up well — can meet the needs of an impressive number of students.

Teaching methods requiring the professor to prepare written or other materials (e.g., case studies, problem-solving exercises, individualized teaching) generally demand a considerable amount of initial work. On the other hand, this inconvenience is often balanced by the quality of learning that these teaching methods promote.

To summarize, remember that you cannot simply choose a teaching method arbitrarily. You must take into account the criteria presented above, as well as the nature of your students, the subject matter, physical and material conditions, and the fit between a method and your personality.

Remember also that the effectiveness of a learning experience depends less on the teaching method than on the quality and quantity of individual intellectual work that it allows students to do.

4.2 Brief Description of Teaching Methods

We now briefly review the principal characteristics of the teaching methods identified and classified in Table 4.1.

4.2.1 Methods Based on Different Forms of Lectures

4.2.1.1 Formal Lectures

Lecture by a Single Instructor. In a lecture — the pre-eminent form of teaching presentation — the professor addresses the students without interruption for the entire class period. He or she may use audio-scripto-visual materials.

During a lecture, students listen quietly, taking notes and watching for indications that underscore the structure of the lecture. The students try to extract the main ideas and analyze their general meaning.

Series of Lectures by Several Instructors. Lectures can be delivered, in the framework of one course, by the same person or by several people, one after the other, during the semester.

4.2.1.2 Informal Presentations

Informal Presentation by the Instructor. In an informal presentation, as in a lecture, the professor addresses the students and constantly maintains control. However, he or she tries to get the students to participate, either by asking them questions or answering their questions. Students can address the professor as well as each other. As in a formal lecture, students take notes, and the professor often uses audio-scripto-visual materials.

Demonstration. The demonstration is a variation of the informal presentation. The professor demonstrates a technique, a process, or an apparatus, instrument, software, etc. The professor uses real objects and, as necessary, the board and transparencies to show things that the students couldn't see otherwise. The professor can perform the demonstration alone or with the help of a student whom he or she guides, step by step.

Generally, students are free to ask questions, but it is difficult for them to take notes.

Case Presentation. The case presentation is another variation of the informal presentation. The professor explains a case to the students, with the goal of proving the validity of a theory presented earlier by applying it to a concrete case — real or simulated. The professor still retains control, even if questions are accepted. He or she may present the case verbally or use slides, transparencies, and audio-visual documents, etc. The professor provides a running commentary on the presentation, while the students take notes and ask questions.

Presentations by Students. Presentations by students are more like a lecture followed by a brief question period than like an informal presentation by the professor. For this type of presentation, the professor generally has divided the content of the course (or the content of supplementary subjects) among the students, who prepare work and present it to their peers. Most of the time they use the board or transparencies. Their classmates rarely take notes.

4.2.2 Methods Favoring Discussion or Group Work

4.2.2.1 Seminars

Classic Seminar. A seminar is composed of weekly meetings of a small group of students (10 to 15) and a professor who plays the role of expert and leader. A seminar allows collective exploration and thorough study of a specialized subject, rather than superficial treatment of all the subjects generally covered in a course. The seminar is characterized by the comprehensive exploration of one subject — a subject broad enough that each student can do specialized research on one specific aspect. A seminar is composed of three essential parts: reading, writing texts, and discussing the content of these texts.

In the first meetings, the professor establishes the common corpus of the basic readings that all the students must do in the weeks to come. In these meetings, the students are each assigned to write a report on one or more texts.

However, the principal objective of these meetings remains the critical discussion of the content of the texts, which all students obviously must read. The professor also corrects the reports presented regularly by each student.

Later in the term, when the basic readings have been finished, the professor asks each student to individually research a particular aspect of the seminar subject. Each student must then do further reading and produce a longer paper in which he or she can use the paper(s) he or she wrote earlier as support. The student gives this long paper to the other students at least one week before discussion, in which the students analyze in detail his or her arguments and conclusions.

Nisbet Propositions. The Nisbet propositions method is a variation of the seminar, with all of its fundamental elements (readings, writing, and discussion) but according to a specific organization.

At the beginning of the term, the professor proposes a list of themes and readings from which each student makes a choice. After doing the selected readings, the student must write six statements (propositions) that he or she will try to have the group adopt.

The members of the group discuss these propositions somewhat like legislators discuss the text of bills.

The quality of the statements is very important: each of them must be clear, concise, and capable of generating discussion; students must therefore exclude obvious facts, pretentious expositions, or unfounded opinions.

The professor allocates to each student three consecutive sessions during the term: two of 90 minutes for debates and one of 10 minutes for the report.

During the first 20 minutes of the "first reading," the student presents his or her six statements, which the class discusses freely during the rest of the session. The goal is to bring forth numerous points of view.

During the "second reading," the discussion is "framed" and must result in the adoption or rejection of each of the six propositions. The propositions that have not been debated in depth are automatically eliminated.

Following the debates, the student must write a detailed report presenting the results and arguments put forward when each of the propositions was adopted or rejected. He or she will try to have that report adopted in the first 10 minutes of the third session. These different texts are recorded in the seminar register with the participants' names.

Debate. The debate is a situation in which the professor engages his or her students in a dialectic process on a given subject. Depending on the situation, the professor assigns a student, a group of students, or half of the students to prepare to argue in favor of a thesis, then assigns another student, another group of students, or the other half of the students to prepare to argue in favor of the opposite thesis, or antithesis.

In a debate, the students do not necessarily have to believe in the thesis or antithesis they champion. A debate is above all an *exercise* of logic and rigor, not a situation in which each participant advances his or her personal values.

The debate requires the presence of a facilitator; usually the professor plays that role. Although a debate must be an exercise, the participants often become emotionally involved. The leader must then mitigate the impact of such emotional involvement and lead the discussion back to the arguments, so that the debate does not degenerate into personal confrontations.

A debate can take one to three sessions of 50 to 60 minutes each. Usually the professor-leader concludes the debate by *synthesizing* the arguments in support of the thesis and the antithesis.

4.2.2.2 Case Studies

Harvard Method. The first case studies date back to the beginning of the century. They began in certain law schools, where students trained in the practice of law by analyzing real cases already decided by the courts. In 1914, the Harvard Business School adopted this method, which has since gained widespread acceptance.

A case is the written presentation of a real problem. In order to be effective, a case must present the students with situations that are very close to those they are living or will have to live. The situations must lead to decisions similar to those they will really have to make.

The situation to be analyzed may include all kinds of real information — facts, events, feelings, expectations, habits, attitudes, the goals of third parties, description of the setting, data, figures, and charts. A case must also have a dramatic side of a certain intensity; its peak must be a point of conflict or urgency requiring a crucial decision. The resolution of the case must not rest on any judgment, any trick, or any prior interpretation of the facts.

The steps in a case study are:

- You give your students the case to study, one week before the discussion, in the form of a document of several pages. You also give them a guide for analyzing the case, and you can suggest certain supplementary readings that may help in their analysis.
- You ask the students to write their analysis of the situation before coming to class.
- Before the discussion, you summarize the case, then ask a volunteer to present his or her analysis.

- The discussion generally begins immediately with the other students, whose analyses converge or diverge.

You remain at all times a non-directive facilitator. Once the students have reached a unanimous decision, you can give your opinion and comment on their analysis of the situation.

Dramatized Case. The dramatized case study is a variation of the Harvard method. It differs only in the manner of presenting the case to the students. In the dramatized case, you do not present the case in writing, but by using video documents, films, tapes, etc.

Simplified Case. The simplified case study is also a variation of the Harvard method, except that the presentation of the case is more succinct.

In the Harvard method, you present the case with a certain number of important and secondary details. The students must exercise their critical skills in considering the details and they absolutely must prepare their study in detail before presenting it in class.

In the simplified case study, on the other hand, you present only the important elements, which makes the initial work easier for the students. That is both an advantage and a disadvantage: because of its brevity, the simplified case can be handed to students just before the discussion; on the other hand, it requires much less analysis from the students.

Pigors Technique. With the Pigors technique — another variation of the Harvard method — you present the case by providing the students only certain minimal information and inviting them to ask you questions to obtain further information. By consulting a notebook in which all of the pieces of information in the case are recorded, you provide only the requested information. The Pigors technique thus allows the students to develop their skills in researching information needed in a case study.

After discussing the information they have collected, the students analyze the case to find one or more solutions, which you compare with the actual solution or the one recommended by experts.

Case Writing by Students. In this variation of the Harvard method, students present a case of their own making to their peers, documented and written according to the classic model of the Harvard method.

Two prerequisites, however, are necessary for the students to build usable cases: first, they must be trained in writing cases; second, they must have some work experience or the equivalent (an internship, for example) in order to write and present real cases and not simply imagined cases.

4.2.2.3 Peer Teaching

Projects. In a course based around a project, you do not give presentations; rather, you supervise the weekly meetings during which the students work on their group project, whether disciplinary or multidisciplinary. The students try to attain the course objectives by doing the assigned project over the term or the year.

Most often the students choose the subject of the project. You can, however, propose a list of subjects when you want to be sure that the students choose a project appropriate to the course objectives, their knowledge, and the imposed time limits.

As strange as it may seem, it is not the subject of a project that is important. It is the application of a method or a body of knowledge to the project, real or otherwise, that really counts. A project requires the students to analyze a problem, propose and apply a solution, and, very often, evaluate that solution.

In the case of a real project, you impose all of the constraints of professional life on the students: calendar, budget limitations, appropriate use of people and resources, and conception of a feasible solution. In the case of a fictitious project, you deliberately eliminate certain constraints (e.g., budget, real client, consequences of the solution) that are not absolutely necessary for the students to attain the course objectives.

At the conclusion of a project, the students usually produce something concrete (e.g., prototype, model, plan of intervention, a written report, or oral presentation).

Problem-Based Learning. In problem-based learning, teams of five to 10 students, whom you supervise, work together for three to six hours each week to solve a large-scale problem that you assign. The rest of the week is then devoted to an independent study generated by the problem. The originality of this method is in that the problem to be solved is a problem for which the students have received no specific training at all.

To solve the problem, students must use the following systematic procedure:

- In groups, they read the problem and find the definitions of terms they do not know.
- They analyze the problem.
- They identify the knowledge they need to acquire to solve the problem.
- They classify this knowledge.

- They establish priorities for research and study (objectives).
- They divide the work.
- They gather material and study individually, according to the established priorities. (This last step takes by far the longest time: 15-20 hours.)

After completing these steps, the students meet again to pool their learning and try to solve the assigned problem. If their work is not satisfactory, they must increase their knowledge before meeting a second time. The students work by themselves, using the documentation at their disposal. When they have solved the problem, they assess what they have learned, then begin a new cycle to try to solve another problem.

In problem-based learning, the crucial step is how you formulate the problems. Each problem must allow the students to attain one or more of the course objectives in question.

With this method, your role is to guide the students in their analysis of the problem. Among other things, you must ascertain that the hypotheses they propose are valid and that the learning objectives they select are appropriate. You can also suggest certain documentary resources to them and question them about their procedure and the solution they propose.

Directed Work or Workshop. In directed work or a workshop, after an initial presentation by the professor, groups of three to five students meet to complete an exercise, a problem, or an assignment before the end of the class period. This activity is on a small scale because the students have little time available. In addition, these exercises are more application exercises than projects involving an ability to systematically solve problems. After this activity, you bring all of the groups together to discuss results.

In directed work, the professor plays the role of a supervisor who allows the groups to work at their own pace and freely gives advice when needed.

Learning Unit. A learning unit is composed of two students who work together for one week. You match the students randomly; the pairs differ from week to week. You can give these pairs two types of assignments.

In one case, all of the students in the class must study the same material and each must prepare about five questions. Then, in class, one member of each pair asks his or her partner a question, and vice versa. If one cannot answer a question, the other plays the role of professor: he or she tries to determine why the teammate does not understand or cannot answer and provides useful explanations. In some difficult cases, the two members can call on the professor to help them solve the problem.

In the second case, half of the students must study the same material and the other half different material. In class, each student must explain to his or her partner what he or she has studied; the partner is free, of course, to ask questions to better understand the explanations. You supervise the session and help pairs that experience difficulties. Sessions with the entire class are optional.

In both cases, it's important for the answers to go beyond simple use of memorization. The answers require at least explanation, application, and analysis.

Simulation. A simulation is a situation during which you reproduce real events to confront students without taking them "into the field."

With computers, professors now possess a powerful and interactive tool to simulate reality for their students. In hydraulics, for example, the computer allows students to simulate complex canalization otherwise inaccessible. Students can then vary at will the arrangement of the components of the system, the delivery, inflow, outflow, and the power of the pumps to solve a given problem — exactly as in reality!

In medicine, students can use a computer to simulate the symptoms of a patient, question the "patient" through software, and interactively arrive at a diagnosis. In other situations, the same medical students can be presented with patients played by actors trained for that purpose or dummies intended for observations, demonstrations, or manipulations.

Finally, in electrical engineering, students can use software to simulate the performance of an electric network or to study overloading, breaks, and the like.

Often, in these domains and numerous others, professors cannot use reality in their courses. Simulation of reality through computers or other means allows students to confront complex situations in the work world, without the constraints of time, risks, and cost.

Educational Game. An educational game has the same characteristics as a parlor game: there are players, rules, and an objective — to win. The difference: the goal of an educational game is to learn.

There are two categories of educational games: games with a structure inspired by existing parlor games (card games, Monopoly®, etc.) and simulation games. Educational games can use all kinds of objects: cards, words, dice, a chessboard, photocopies, slides, posters, matrices. They may bring together individuals or teams or they may confront one person with a task and certain constraints (time limit, moves, regulations, etc.).

According to the structure of educational games, the specific objectives can vary considerably. For example, in a game we designed, "Play on Words," the professor hands a packet of 18 similar diamond-shaped cards to teams of four or five people. On each of these cards, a phrase describes one step in the systematic preparation of a course. The members of each team must discuss and agree on the ideal order of these steps. Once each team reaches a consensus, the professor asks the teams to compare their results. Figure 4.1 (on the next page) shows the cards, in no particular order.

In another game, entitled "Cloudy," the participants learn to use various types of clouds to identify different meteorological phenomena. Students play this game individually, using a guide, sketches, and slides.

Role Play. In role play, you call on several students to perform for their classmates a short scene composed of real-life situations. You do not provide any text, just different sets of general directions. Each student improvises, trying to enter into his or her character — feelings, behaviors, and attitudes.

Once the role play has ended, the professor asks the "actors" to tell what they felt at one moment or another and to be specific about why they adopted a certain behavior. Afterwards, the discussion gets under way with the "spectators."

You can use role play, for example, with law students, who might try a hypothetical case in what is called a moot court. Taking turns, the students play the role of judge, prosecutor, defense lawyer, plaintiff, etc.

You can use role play in other disciplines as well: for example, to simulate therapeutic interviews in social service, medicine, and psychology. They are also used to simulate interviews for selecting candidates, negotiating meetings, and so forth.

4.2.2.4 Other Methods

Laboratory Session. A laboratory session is practical work that students perform following a lecture, and during which they use various instruments: test tubes, microscopes, oscilloscopes, computers, robots, etc. The objective is to learn and master the experimental method — to plan an experiment, verify hypotheses, take measurements, analyze results, and put it all into a written report.

In a laboratory session, students are placed into groups of two to five so that they can participate actively in the task. Generally, to help your stu-

Figure 4.1 Basic Materials for "Play on Words" Game

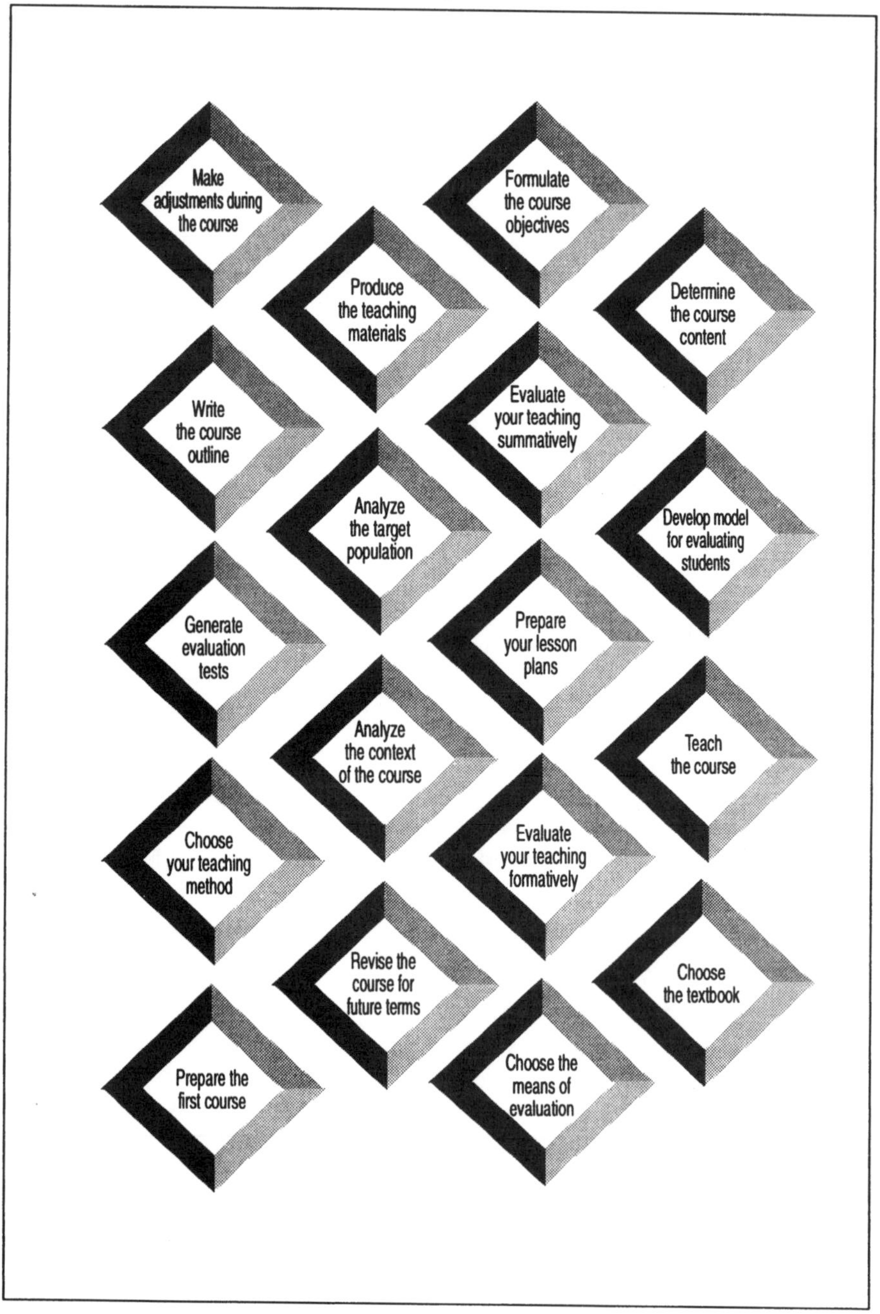

dents prepare for a session, you should provide them with a laboratory guide that specifies the objectives and describes the instruments at their disposal, the necessary preparation, the steps for them to complete, and the form of their final report. It can also contain brief theoretical reminders.

Micro-teaching. Although micro-teaching is mainly used to train teachers, the principle can easily be extended to other disciplines, such as nursing care (assistance with a patient) and sports training (learning precise movements).

With micro-teaching, future teachers learn to master a certain number of communication skills:

- introducing a subject,
- emphasizing the structure in a lecture,
- varying their voice, gestures, and expressions,
- using positive reinforcement,
- asking questions, and
- answering questions.

To develop these pedagogical skills, each future teacher gives a micro-lesson (10-15 minutes) to a micro-group of five or six students in front of several colleagues. The micro-lesson is recorded on videotape. Then the student teacher, his or her classmates, and the professor immediately view the video, which they stop when necessary to make comments.

Every week, all of the future teachers practice a different communication skill. At the end of the year, each of them teaches a complete lesson (50 minutes), during which he or she tries to use all of the communication skills harmoniously.

Team Teaching. In team teaching, two or more professors from the same discipline or complementary disciplines work together to teach a course.

This method applies to presentations given alternately by two professors during the same course hour — presentations during which they give students complementary elements of information. It also applies to more active teaching situations, such as projects, debates, and case studies.

In team teaching, the professors write the course objectives, choose the learning activities, and determine the means of evaluation by dividing the tasks. Team teaching requires frequent meetings, so that each professor is involved in the direction chosen by the team.

4.2.3 Methods Based on Individual Learning

The teaching methods presented below all have one point in common: a lasting and steady individual relationship between a professor and a student. You do not teach a course to each student; you supervise the students' development. In a way, you play the role of counselor or director of studies, to guide the individual pedagogical evolution of the students, who discuss with you the tasks to be completed.

With teaching methods based on individual learning, the progress made by each student is different.

4.2.3.1 Guided Work

Learning Contract. A learning contract is a teaching method based on the principle of negotiation between professor and student. This negotiation can focus on the learning objectives, activities that lead to attainment of these objectives, and the means and criteria for evaluation.

At the beginning of a course, you present the general course objectives to the students. Then, each student drafts a learning contract that reflects his or her interests for the course. This contract contains:

- more specific objectives (which must, of course, be in accord with the general course objectives);
- activities likely to help the student attain these objectives;
- a calendar;
- suggested methods of evaluation;
- possibly the grade the student hopes to obtain, in exchange for work of quality that meets your requirements.

Each student gives you his or her contract; the two of you discuss the objectives, activities, calendar, and evaluation, sharing your viewpoints.

Given that it is recommended, for practical reasons, that you divide the initial learning contract into intermediary contracts of a lesser scope — which allow the student a greater feeling for his or her progress — you and the student agree on one or several contracts. You also plan to meet at certain stages, so that you will be able to judge the work accomplished and perhaps provide constructive advice.

Reading Program. As the name indicates, a reading program is a teaching method in which you give each student the responsibility to cover certain readings. All of the readings, as well as the activities connected with them, must allow him or her to attain the course objectives.

When you first meet with your students, you evaluate the interests or needs of each and propose a series of readings for him or her, some of which are obligatory. The student must then read the suggested texts and synthesize them in writing, in the form of simple informative summaries, critical summaries, or essays. To verify that each student is reading and understanding, you plan several meetings over the course of the term.

Training Period. The training period is a session of practical experience that you set for a student, usually in a place similar to his or her future work environment.

The length and forms of training periods vary considerably according to professions and academic programs. In some cases, students go for training once or twice a week; in others, the training period takes place at the end of the term.

During the training, you entrust the student with attaining certain practical objectives. The student logs the outstanding facts of his or her training in a daily notebook, mentioning the results of his or her work, noting his or her thoughts, analyzing the relations that exist between his or her studies and the practical experience, and describing how he or she is solving professional difficulties.

In addition to being advised by a professor, the trainee is always placed under the tutelage of a supervisor from the professional milieu. These two counselors have complementary roles: the supervisor provides several formative evaluations of the student, while the two jointly provide the final summative evaluation. The two might use a shared criteria evaluation grid, taking into account the training report produced by the student.

At the conclusion of the training, the student usually must turn in a training report in which he or she has recorded the overall results of the experience and evaluated the quality of the training.

Cooperative Teaching. In cooperative teaching, the student alternates theoretical courses and training periods in a firm (or the equivalent). There are various formats.

The student first takes courses for one or two terms. Then, he or she leaves the institution to undergo intensive training in the selected firm. This training lasts several months and the trainee receives a salary.

Intensive teaching and intensive training alternate several times during the cooperative experience.

In cooperative education, the same pedagogical organization exists as in classic training — a supervisor from the educational institution, a supervisor from the host firm, and a report at the end of the training period.

4.2.3.2 Individual Work

Modular Teaching. In modular teaching, the content of a course is divided into a certain number of units, called learning modules. A module consists of four required elements developed by the professor: a pre-test, objectives, learning activities, and a post-test.

Before starting a learning module, the student takes a pre-test to evaluate his or her mastery of the knowledge prerequisite to that module as well as his or her knowledge concerning the content of the module. Depending on the results of the pre-test, the student must do part or all of the learning activities of the module. The student who passes the pre-test is exempt from these activities; he or she can then prepare for the following module and take the corresponding pre-test.

Following the pre-test, the student must complete different learning activities that the professor assigns or that he or she chooses. These can be readings and individual studies, group activities, or extracurricular activities. You give the student a notebook containing the corrected copy of the pre-test and the interpretation of the questions, the list of general and specific objectives, and instructions for the readings and the procedure to follow.

The student works independently on the activities, consulting you in case of difficulties. Then, when the student believes he or she has mastered the objectives of the module, he or she takes the post-test. If the student passes, he or she goes on to the next module; if not, the student must start the module over and take the post-test again. This process is repeated several times if necessary.

However, in order to encourage students to prepare appropriately and not simply try to make it past the multiple-choice questions that are most often used in this type of individualized teaching, some institutions impose penalties on students who do not pass a module on their first try.

Audio-Tutorial. The audio-tutorial is a variation of the modular teaching developed by S.N. Postlethwait in 1961.

However, in contrast with traditional modular teaching, the audio-tutorial consists of whole-class sessions, activities in groups of seven or eight students, and instructions on cassettes (for the individual activities). The name of this teaching method derives from that aspect, in which the professor uses an audio recording to play the role of tutor.

Each week, the professor presents the class with its objectives. Then, each student begins an individual study program, guided by the professor's recording. The professor gives mainly information and instructions for the activities, but can also provide encouragement and an overview of the study material.

Students can work and study in a learning resource center, which offers them, at their convenience, all of the resource material they might need. A professor is also there to help out as necessary.

In addition, to break the monotony of solitary work, when all of the students have completed their work, they gather to listen to a presentation, watch a film, and so forth. They can also, in small groups, do research, experiments, tasks, or projects.

At the end of the week, the professor meets with each group to evaluate the students on their attainment of the objectives for the week. The first part of the evaluation is oral (30 minutes), the second in writing (15 minutes).

Individually Prescribed Instruction (IPI). The originality of individually prescribed instruction stems from the following principal characteristics:

- The professor writes and organizes all of the specific learning objectives for each course. (This can also be done by a group of professors.)
- The professor designs and develops the different pedagogical tools to help students attain these objectives.
- The professor designs and develops a battery of tests to determine the proficiency of each student. Sometimes this evaluation occurs at the start of the course, sometimes at different points throughout the term.
- The professor designs and develops a battery of pre-tests to measure attainment of specific objectives of each learning unit.
- The professor regularly updates each student on his or her progress and suggests ways ("prescriptions") to attain the objectives partially attained or to continue along his or her way.

Each student benefits from a thorough analysis of his or her profile at the beginning of the course. You propose ("prescribe") a procedure and individual activities so that he or she attains, in a definite order, all of the objectives of the course. The students take pre-tests before starting each of the short learning units that you have individually "prescribed." Because these units are short, you meet frequently with your students. Furthermore, a cumulative dossier allows you to follow the evolution of each student.

Personalized System of Instruction (PSI). The personalized system of instruction (also called the Keller Plan, from the name of its author, F.S. Keller, 1965) is based on the following characteristics:

- The course content is divided into small units.
- A work guide provides the student with the objectives to attain, instructions, and a list of the documents necessary for his or her learning.
- The student has frequent contact with several people other than the professor — assistants assigned to help teach, correct the tests at the conclusion of each unit, etc.

At the beginning of the semester, each student receives a document describing the course. His or her work is divided into units, with an individual learning experience, a project, or exercises required. Each unit is followed by a test; a student can, on the average, take two or three tests per week; you correct each test in his or her presence and comment on the results.

Students can take the tests an unlimited number of times, in principle, with no effect on the final grade. The student can start the following unit only if he or she has sufficiently mastered the knowledge in the preceding unit (with a grade of 80%, for example). The final test, however, is the same for all students.

Distance Learning. Distance learning is a form of instruction that has evolved from what used to be called "correspondence courses."

In a course based on this teaching method, the student works alone, away from campus, most often at home.

After registering for the course, the student receives the course documents by mail. In most cases, a written guide indicates what work he or she must accomplish using these documents.

These documents, prepared by the professor or team of professors, are for the most part written, since audio-visual documents, computer materials, or other materials are expensive to produce and difficult to distribute or circulate.

After completing the work, the student mails it to the institution, where graders correct and grade it.

In some cases, the student can periodically consult with a professor in a regional center; in other cases, he or she can obtain, at predetermined times, a telephone consultation with a professor.

Programmed Teaching. Programmed teaching is a teaching method that strictly applies the notion of learning conditioning proposed by B.F. Skinner (stimulus → response → reinforcement). Programmed teaching is a written text punctuated with hundreds of questions (stimuli) for which the student provides answers (responses), which he or she verifies (reinforcement — positive or negative).

To develop a teaching program, you draft and organize all of the specific objectives of the course, then develop appropriate work "programs" that allow students to attain these objectives. These programs take the form of custom texts interrupted here and there by hundreds of questions. The student compares each of his or her answers with answers furnished by the program: if the answer is correct, the student continues; if it is wrong, he or she starts again.

There are two types of programs: linear and branched. A linear program imposes the same progression on all of the students. A branched program proposes, according to the students' answers, certain loops of supplemental learning that allow the student to either review material that he or she inadequately understood or supplement that material.

Review

Three Categories of Teaching Methods

- Teaching methods based on *different forms of presentations.*
- Methods focusing on *discussion or group work.*
- Methods based on *individual learning.*

General Conclusions on Teaching Methods

- There is no *best* teaching method.
- All teaching methods are equivalent when the objectives are simple, such as the acquisition and comprehension of knowledge.
- Teaching methods that are more "student-centered" especially help students attain objectives associated with long-term memorization, thought development, development of motivation, and learning transfer.
- The superior results obtained with certain teaching methods are apparently less attributable to these methods themselves than to the quantity and quality of personal intellectual work they engender.

Criteria for Selecting Teaching Methods

- Levels of cognitive objectives targeted.
- Capacity to promote autonomous and continuous learning.
- Degree of control exercised by the student.
- Number of students a method can accommodate.
- Number of hours of preparation, student contact, and correction required.

Factors Influencing the Effectiveness of a Teaching Method

- Nature of the students.
- Number of students.
- Material taught.
- Instructor's personality.
- Physical and material conditions.
- Targeted objectives.

CHAPTER 5

CHOOSING YOUR TEACHING MATERIALS

Teaching materials are the media or technical objects that facilitate the communication of information between professor and students. In this chapter, we treat the most commonly used teaching materials, which can be grouped into five categories: written, scripto-visual, audio-visual, audio, and computer (Table 5.1).

Table 5.1 Teaching materials most often used

Written	Scripto-Visual	Audio-Visual	Audio	Computer
Textbook Duplicated course notes Photocopies	Blackboard Transparencies Slides	Video Film Slides synchronized with sound track	Audiotape	Educational software Application software

In Table 5.1, we have intentionally omitted materials seldom or never used in postsecondary instruction: 8 mm loops, filmstrips, records, radios, photographs, videodiscs, three-dimensional objects, maps, models, and posters.

In this chapter, we first analyze the underlying reasons for using teaching materials. Then, we evaluate the effects of these materials on learning. Finally, we offer some practical advice on the appropriate use of the materials discussed here.

5.1 Underlying Reasons for Using Teaching Materials

Usually a professor uses a given teaching material simply when he or she feels the need and when this material is available. In fact, every professor at some time is confronted with the need to use something other than voice or gesture. Quite naturally, then, he or she will look for other materials that will enhance teaching.

5.2 Influence of Teaching Materials on Learning

Let us state quite frankly that there is no pedagogy of teaching materials — no blackboard pedagogy, map pedagogy, or computer pedagogy. Teaching materials are only tools, with no other influence on pedagogy than that given by the professor using them. They have no specific pedagogical virtue; they only serve to extend the professor's pedagogical actions. That's why their pedagogical effectiveness is directly proportional to that of the professor who conceives and uses them.

Given that many professors are tempted to use the latest teaching materials on the market (computers, videodiscs, etc.) and that others, in contrast, remain faithful to more traditional materials, (textbooks, transparencies, etc.), we will now try to determine which materials help improve teaching and, ultimately, learning.

To do this, we will analyze the four *propositions* stemming from research on using teaching materials in class (see Richard Clark and G. Salomon, "Media in Teaching," in the bibliography):

1. No teaching material is better than any other for a given learning task.
2. In a learning situation where materials are used, improvements are rarely attributable solely to the material.
3. In a learning situation where materials are used, the quality of learning depends at least as much on the students' motivation to learn with the material used as on the material itself.
4. Simple, inexpensive teaching materials are preferable to complex, expensive materials.

First Proposition: No teaching material is better than any other for a given learning task.

The results of research on using teaching materials in class have not been able to prove the superiority of any one medium. On the contrary, it seems that all teaching materials can be equally effective toward most pedagogical objectives. In fact, learning seems to be influenced more by the content than by the material.

In terms of pedagogical effectiveness, then, choosing materials for a new course is simple: use whatever materials are available!

Second Proposition: In a learning situation where materials are used, improvements are rarely attributable solely to the material.

Since the end of World War II, each decade has brought to the world of education new, more promising teaching materials: films, audio-visual aids, television, micro-computers, and videodiscs.

People always believed that these new materials could significantly improve learning. However, when we analyze results again, we discover that the improvements in question are probably attributable more to overall improvement in the teaching situation than to the new material.

In addition, results prove that a new teaching material does not automatically improve a learning situation. At the very most, the novelty of the material may increase student motivation to learn, which leads to the ascertained positive effects.

Third Proposition: In a learning situation where materials are used, the quality of the learning depends at least as much on the students' motivation to learn with the material used as on the material itself.

It seems that the improvements students *believe* or *hope* to make using instructional materials are at least as important to learning as the material itself. It's not necessarily the material that makes a difference, but rather the students' opinion of the value of this material: their intellectual effort is proportional to their perception of the importance and appropriateness of the task and the material.

For example, if students believe that you are using a lot of transparencies just to save time, and if they conclude that you just want to "stuff their heads," the transparencies become ineffective, no matter how carefully prepared. Moreover, if you show a film to illustrate an important aspect of the course content, but the students view it more as recreation than instruction, the film becomes less effective.

So when you want to use teaching materials, you must take student attitudes into account. You should at least present the materials you've chosen and explain their advantages, to involve your students in the proposed task. If it seems that you are poorly integrating these materials or otherwise using them improperly or artificially, they will automatically become less effective.

Fourth Proposition: Simple, inexpensive teaching materials are preferable to complex, expensive materials.

Since no one teaching material is better than any other, it makes sense to use less expensive materials, but only if they actually help students in the cognitive operations required by the learning task. You cannot, for example, require of the blackboard the power and flexibility of the computer; on the other hand, in certain cases, simple transparencies with overlaps can be as effective as a film, at much less expense.

5.3 Practical Advice

To gain the expected instructional benefits from whatever materials you choose, you must use them appropriately. In the following pages we review the teaching materials listed in Table 5.1 and provide practical advice on using each of them.

5.3.1 Written Materials

The written materials at your disposal are the textbook, duplicated course notes, and photocopies, which can be used separately or together.

5.3.1.1 Textbook

Generally, a professor chooses a textbook for a given course because that textbook covers the content of the course, in large part or completely. This required textbook allows students to reread and study, out of class, material presented in class.

You can use a textbook in three ways:

- Follow the textbook page by page;
- Treat only the important points from each chapter (principles, key ideas, etc.) and give examples not necessarily from the textbook;
- Cover the content in a certain way, while the textbook presents it in a different way.

Each of these approaches has its advantages and disadvantages. We will analyze them separately.

First Approach. When you follow the textbook page by page, it seems to help the students. They always know where you are, they don't need to take as many notes, and they have in hand all of the illustrations and your detailed organization.

With this approach, however, the students are only more or less passive recipients. They also tend to believe that, after your lecture, they have understood everything, and that the very fact of attending class allows them to learn. Logically, then, they think it's useless to reread the textbook and study regularly. They believe they can simply consult the textbook before the test.

In order to learn, students must process information, go over it again, transpose it, extrapolate from it, summarize the essential elements, test their understanding through exercises, or at least answer questions often found in a textbook at the end of the chapters. If they do not regularly engage in such activities, they will learn less and have poorer long-term memorization.

With this first approach, what you do in class corresponds in full to the book's content.

Second Approach. When you cover only the important points of the textbook, you can more thoroughly present what is essential. When you leave it up to your students to cover the details, you have more time in class to explain carefully and in depth the aspects you consider essential and even present new examples, in addition to those in the textbook. You can also ask the students questions and answer theirs.

With this second approach, the students are theoretically more intellectually active; they need to remain attentive, because you are not covering the textbook content word for word. What's more, you are not necessarily covering the content of the chapter according to the order used in the textbook. The students who want to understand and write down your logical connections, explanations, and sequences must remain intellectually alert.

After class, students have the impression that the textbook offers them additional content that will help them build on what they have retained from your presentation. Moreover, you will probably recommend to them, as you lecture, to study some passage that they are not covering in class.

Furthermore, you provide a personal synthesis that will help alert students to read the textbook in a more enlightened way.

With this second approach, you will cover less content in class than presented in the textbook, but more in depth. Through your synthesis and examples, you transcend the textbook's content without diverging from it.

Third Approach. When you cover the same material as the textbook, but in an entirely different way, your treatment deviates from the textbook's. Your objective with this approach is not to repeat what the author of the textbook states, but to compare your own vision with that of another authority. You and the textbook take two parallel paths through the same content.

Whatever your approach, a textbook must be read to be worthwhile. It's difficult to get students to read; yet if the task seems pertinent to them, they read willingly. In Recommendations 5.1 (on the next page), we offer some advice to help you encourage your students to read.

5.3.1.2 Duplicated Course Notes

If you cannot find an appropriate textbook, you can provide duplicated course notes for your students. These notes can take either of two forms: complete text (like a textbook) or incomplete text (like an outline).

Complete Text. In this form, you present the information as in a textbook. The text is well-structured. Each chapter is written in full sentences. The material is explained and the figures and tables are accompanied by commentary. Duplicated notes differ from textbooks only in typography. The notes are used in class as a textbook (Section 5.3.1.1).

If you are teaching a course for the first time, don't write complete-text course notes; such a project requires hundreds of hours, which could be better spent preparing other instructional activities.

Recommendations 5.1 Textbook

- Point out to the students, from the beginning of the term, how you plan to use the textbook in class, and insist on the importance of personal daily study.
- Repeat the above advice regularly during the term.
- Indicate, during your lectures, the page numbers or figures that support what you're presenting.
- Give students, at the end of each class, precise instructions concerning the pages to read.
- Assign the students tasks requiring reading: answering a question, establishing a comparison between two points of view, on researching an application of the theory.
- Work with the reading assignments at least once a week, in some way, as long as it reinforces students' study of the textbook: answering questions, debating questions asked during the preceding session, having students do question-and-answer work in pairs (see Chapter 4), etc.
- Solicit questions from the students about their readings, either verbally during class or in writing, before the following class. This permits you to check them and answer the most important questions later in class.
- Ask your students, during the term, what they think of the textbook. This allows those who have been reading the textbook to confirm its value. It may also encourage those who have not been reading it to do so.
- Ask your students, at least once or twice per term, about their reading and studying habits; if they are not regular, try to improve them.
- Invite your students to use all of the resources of the textbook — table of contents, index, bibliography, glossary, problems or questions at the end of the chapters, summaries, etc. A good textbook is a textbook that the students use frequently.

Incomplete Text. In this form, you present the information as an outline. It is not exhaustive. You must complete it through lectures, during which the students take notes. This form of duplicated notes serves as a framework for you and your students. You organize the elements as you plan to cover them in the course, but you present them very succinctly — detailed table of contents for each chapter (which facilitates note-taking), definitions, important formulas, key words, lists, copies of transparencies used in the course, etc.

Incomplete text course notes are a memory tool, of little value to anyone who tries to read them without having attended the lectures.

Such duplicated course notes are thus a palliative used in the absence of a real textbook. It is an acceptable temporary measure; however, the conscientious professor will quickly locate a textbook. If you cannot find one, write one — spreading the project out over several years, of course.

Recommendations 5.2 Duplicated Course Notes

- Explain to the students, at the beginning of the term, how to use the duplicated course notes with the lectures.
- Repeat the above explanation several times during the term.
- When you lecture, indicate the relevant page numbers or illustrations.
- If you provide incomplete course notes, do not make a practice of leaving blank space for taking notes, for two reasons:
    1. students naturally do not like to pay for "blank pages";
    2. when you limit the students to filling in blank spaces, you undermine their intellectual activity.
- Continue searching for a real textbook, because students keep duplicated course notes for a few months at most. After the course, they forget this type of document, while a textbook remains a resource that they keep in their libraries.

5.3.1.3 Photocopies

Photocopies are used so often that we no longer know if they are a blessing or a curse. For each course, a student may receive 50-100 photocopies of all kinds: course outline, articles, keys for tests and exercises, instructions, copies of transparencies, test copies, and so on. At the end of the course, all of these photocopies go directly into the wastebasket or a folder to be shelved. So think twice before distributing photocopies.

Sometimes photocopies are essential. Texts that students exchange during a seminar, for example, or short texts (one or two pages) that supplement a project or intellectual work are often photocopied.

Recommendations 5.3 Photocopies

- Present photocopied documents clearly and systematically:
    - Give a title to each document, prominently placed at the top of the first page.
    - Staple all photocopied documents together as a single packet.
    - Number the documents (document No. 1, document No. 2, and so on) and paginate continuously (page 1, page 2, and so on).
    - Be consistent in your photocopying: single-sided or double-sided
    - Be careful with the visual aspect: quality reproduction; letters and numbers easily legible; layout with sufficient space; title, pagination, and references in a conspicuous position.
- Limit the number of documents photocopied. Each document must fill an essential function.
- Make sure not to violate copyright laws.

However, you should avoid using photocopies systematically; they should be only occasional complements to more comprehensive and basic course texts. If you are in the habit of just handing out photocopies to your students, you should consider a compromise: put together one single handout, complete or incomplete, in which you organize cohesively the content that you presented in previous terms in the form of photocopies.

5.3.2 Scripto-Visual Materials

5.3.2.1 Blackboard

When you use the board, do it skillfully. Learn to write on it legibly and systematically, so that the results are not an incomprehensible scribble.

Recommendations 5.4 Blackboard

- Write large and dark enough so that your writing can be read from the back of the class.
- Use the entire surface of the board, not just the same area all of the time.
- Write your lecture outline on the board, at the beginning of the class, and refer to it each time you reach a new point. Each item in the outline must consist of only a few words.
- Work at the board in sections: first fill the section furthest to the left, then fill the next section to the right, and so forth. This allows you to keep the information on the board for a certain time and makes it easier for your students to take notes.
- Once the board is filled, erase first the sections furthest to the left, after making sure that the students have finished writing down the contents.
- Make sure that your movements as you write on the board are appropriate:
  - After filling one section, move to the right, so that you don't hide the information from the students.
  - Use a pointer of adequate length to reach any section of the board without standing in front of it.
  - Turn and face your students frequently to maintain visual contact with them.
  - Do not write everything you and your students say: it takes too much time and is useless. Limit yourself to what is essential.
  - Stop regularly to verify, with questions or other means, that students understand. Otherwise students will spend most of their time transcribing rather than thinking.

5.3.2.2 Transparencies

You can use transparencies to outline the basic points of your presentation: to display, for example, a simplified illustration, diagrams, cross-sections, key words summarizing the different parts of a development, or an outline of your lesson plans. Transparencies present a notable advantage over the board: they can be prepared in advance, saving you and your students an appreciable amount of time and energy in class. Again, however, you must use them properly.

Recommendations 5.5 Transparencies

- Be "visual" in designing your transparencies: vary the arrangement, colors, and forms.
- Limit the text to 15 lines.
- Limit the number of transparencies you use in one class period (10-15 maximum).
- Write in tall, wide, and legible characters. If you use typewritten or printed characters, use a photocopy machine to enlarge them 300%. If you write by hand, make your letters large enough to read.
- Use a system for arranging and numbering your transparencies so that you can find them quickly and easily in class. For example, punch the transparencies and arrange them in a binder, separated by blank sheets of paper; place them in a box or folder; or mount them on numbered frames.
- Use a pointer at least one foot long to indicate information on the screen. Use a pointed object (a sharp pencil or a swizzle stick) to show it directly on the transparency, so that you don't to block the screen.
- Maintain visual contact with the students by turning toward the screen only when necessary.

5.3.2.3 Slides

It's not very easy to use slides, because the room must be dark. In the dark, you have only your voice and the projected image to hold the students' attention. In addition, students cannot easily take notes in the dark, and slide presentations can become tedious if they last too long.

Recommendations 5.6 Slides

- Present the slides at an opportune time — not at the end of class to make your work easier, but at the moment when they should accompany a given explanation.
- Comment on each slide and describe its content. Do not rely on the old line, "As you can see, ..."
- Limit your slide presentations to 10 minutes per hour. Choose only the most pertinent slides, because it's useless to show slides just for the pleasure of showing them.
- Contextualize the objects that you present, in order of decreasing size, going from wide shots to close-ups.
- Before you show the slides, focus the students' attention on your primary points.

5.3.3 Audio-Visual Materials

Audio-visual documents usually allow you to bring to class a reality otherwise inaccessible to students: geographic sites, sea beds, microscopic photos, animated images, testimonies, radio or TV broadcasts, phenomena, and events of all kinds.

Recommendations 5.7 Audio-Visual Materials

- View the material before presenting it to students.
- If there's a guide to using the material, read it and plan a way to integrate the material into the class.
- Tell the students, in advance, about your objective in using the material. Tell them what to expect and how long the presentation will take. Draw their attention to the important elements. Relate the material to the course content (past and future). And specify what you will expect of the students following the presentation.
- If it would take too long to present the material in its entirety, show only part of it.
- Show the important sequences twice, so that the students can see things that they missed the first time. Do not hesitate to interrupt the presentation to comment on a particular image.
- Do not require students to take notes during the presentation, because they could miss something important.
- Do not use audio-visual materials excessively in any course.

5.3.4 Audio Materials

There are some courses in which it may be appropriate to play recorded material (such as voices, music, and other sounds). Although recordings are most often used in modern language courses, professors in other disciplines may also use them for interviews, speeches, and musical or theatrical productions.

Furthermore, with certain teaching methods (audio-tutorials, for example), the professor is partly replaced by a cassette that gives individual instructions to each student.

Recommendations 5.8 Audio Materials

- Use quality recordings, because students quickly tire of listening to something that's difficult to hear.
- Do not use recordings that are too long, because listening requires of the students an intense effort of concentration that you must not underestimate.

5.3.5 Computer Software

Use of instructional computer software falls into two categories: educational software and application software.

5.3.5.1 Educational Software

Educational software is specifically designed for teaching a certain body of knowledge in a given discipline.

An educational program is usually structured in branches; it interacts with the user through menus and dialogues. Many professors have a growing appreciation of educational software because the programs allow interaction, develop initiative, and individualize teaching of contents as well as underlying cognitive developments. In addition, educational software can be created in all fields of knowledge.

However, an educational program has a *fixed structure* predetermined by its author, which prevents the user from creating anything new. It serves *exclusively* to help students acquire and master knowledge.

Recommendations 5.9 Educational Software

- Evaluate the program before putting it into the hands of students. First judge its instructional qualities, then its technical qualities.
- Verify how much the content of the program and the objectives it allows students to attain conform to those of the course.
- Evaluate the quality of the interaction provided by the program.
- Read the documentation that accompanies the program, for both the professor and the students.
- Verify whether the program is flexible enough to allow individualization of instruction in the course material and fosters underlying cognitive developments.
- Check whether the program is easy and enjoyable to use.
- Plan how to integrate the program into the instructional activities of the course.
- Plan how to evaluate what the students learn using the program.
- Evaluate the compatibility of the program with the available hardware.
- Precisely plan how your students will use the program: place, dates, length of time, and logistics.
- Determine whether extra staff will be necessary.
- Evaluate the cost of purchasing copies of a program or licenses necessary to make copies. (Pirating of software is a criminal offense.)
- Test the program on a small scale before using it with the entire class.
- Never design a course solely around individual use of educational software; students need much more than a machine to learn and persevere.

5.3.5.2 Application Software

Application software helps students do work that traditionally has been done by hand. As with any tool, the students must first familiarize themselves with this type of software. There are programs for architectural or mechanical design, various accounting operations, word processing, desktop publishing, and so forth.

Recommendations 5.10 Application Software

A. Before having students use application software:

- Do not let students train themselves by trial and error. It usually results in a loss of time and motivation. It's better to plan solid training for your students (see part B below).
- Plan what the students should learn in this training.
- Evaluate the instructional and technical qualities of the application software in question (Recommendations 5.9). To do so, evaluate its content and objectives, as well as the documentation that accompanies it, and plan how to integrate the software into course activities.
- Evaluate the adaptability of the application software to your planned teaching needs.
- Examine the possibility of adding to the examples of the application software some examples directly linked to the course.

B. To train students to use application software:

- First, give students a general overview of the possibilities of the software, perhaps using a schematic representation of all of its functions. Explain the main functions and the underlying concepts, without entering into the procedures or forms of interaction.
- Second, demonstrate the software with a demonstration file or a demonstration scenario. Depending on the size of the group, work with an individual screen, a giant screen and a projector intended for demonstrations, or a control system for the screens (as is done in a language laboratory with tapes).

  Note: If no appropriate equipment is available, simply skip the demonstration and settle for a good general presentation of the software and a quality guided tour of its features.
- Third, let your students explore the software, using a "minimal manual" that you design. This manual should consist of a series of exercises focusing on your subject area. The exercises should be of increasing difficulty with only minimal explanations of the software itself. A "minimal manual" is based on the fact that the users of a new software want to quickly perform a concrete task, without having to read a thick user manual. The "minimal manual" should refer frequently, at appropriate moments, to the official user manual.
- Fourth, ask students to complete projects of a broad scope that require them to use all of the software functions. Only at this time should you hand them the official user manual.

Application software, unlike educational software, has an *open structure that favors multiple uses*. Application software allows students to perform a multitude of cognitive operations: making professional decisions, doing forecasts and projections, performing calculations, analyzing the results of these calculations, and making corrections.

Application software is usually produced by private firms for the benefit of professionals in various disciplines.

Review

Influence of Teaching Materials on Learning

- Materials — audio-scripto-visual, written, and computer — have no particular pedagogical virtue. They are only an extension of the professor; they are pedagogically only as effective as the professor who uses them.
- No teaching material is better than any other for a given learning task.
- In a learning situation, improvements are rarely attributable solely to the teaching material used.
- In a learning situation, the quality of learning depends at least as much on the students' motivation to learn with the material used as on the material itself.
- Simple, inexpensive teaching materials are preferable to complex, expensive materials.

Practical Advice

Written Materials

- You can use a textbook or complete course packet in three ways:

  - follow it page by page;

  - treat only the important points;

  - cover the content in a different way than in the textbook.
- Do not use incomplete duplicated course notes for years; replace them as soon as possible with a complete packet of course notes or a textbook.
- Avoid relying on photocopies systematically. Use them as occasional complements.

Scripto-Visual Materials

- Work at the board legibly and systematically, taking care to maintain visual contact with the students.
- The principal advantage of transparencies is that they allow you to synthesize information; it is useless to use a lot of them or to use them improperly.
- Slide presentations must be short because of the darkness required.

Audio-Visual Materials

- Audio-visual materials must absolutely be integrated into your teaching. View the materials before presenting them. Explain what the students should observe and what you expect of them from the presentation.

Audio Materials

- Instructional use of sound recordings is limited. They can provide a useful and inexpensive means to reproduce and analyze all kinds of interviews.

Computer Software

- The use of computer software — educational programs and applications — must not constitute an end in itself.

CHAPTER 6

DETAILED COURSE PLANNING

Once you have determined your objectives and chosen your teaching methods, materials, and evaluation instruments, you can establish a detailed weekly chronological sketch of all the course activities.

To do this, you can use the *course syllabus*, which we discuss in Section 6.1. With the course syllabus, you can organize, in matrix form, week after week, all of the contents and instructional activities of the course.

The course syllabus is related to another document, the *course outline*, which we present in Section 6.2. The course outline is a text you hand out during the first class. In it, you describe in detail the organization of the course.

In Section 6.3, we discuss a third document that will help you prepare each class, the *lesson plan*.

Finally, in Section 6.4, we discuss preparing for the very important first class, when you meet your students and distribute the course outline.

6.1 Planning the Course Syllabus

The course syllabus is a planning tool in the form of a matrix in which you try to record and synchronize the content and activities of the entire course.

You can more easily determine the amount of time to allot to the different contents in the course syllabus if you have already assigned them degrees of priority and difficulty (Table 1.1).

6.1.1 Basic Structure of the Course Syllabus

In Table 6.1, we propose a basic structure for the course syllabus, divided into four headings. It could, of course, be divided differently, depending on the number of instructional components you plan and your way of planning them.

You indicate the week numbers in the first column and the contents to cover each week, as well as the corresponding activities, in the second column. Developing a satisfactory course syllabus will require several drafts, because the first distribution of the contents and activities is rarely perfect.

In the third column, you list the different types of work the students must do at home each week to attain the course objectives — pages or chapters to read in the textbook, numbers of exercises to do, titles of laboratory sessions, assignments to do, steps of a project, and so forth.

Make sure that the number of hours needed for these weekly activities is in line with the norms at your institution. Generally, two hours of work outside of class correspond to one class hour; consequently, for a three-credit course (45 class hours), you can require about 90-100 hours of outside work over the term.

In the fourth column, across from the corresponding weeks, you note test dates and due dates for assignments, exercises, progress reports, laboratory work, etc.

Table 6.1 Basic Structure of the Course Syllabus

COURSE SYLLABUS			
Week	Weekly content and activities	Students' weekly work	Evaluation
1			
2			
3			
4			
...			
15			

6.1.2 Examples

To illustrate the preceding discussion, we now offer two examples of course syllabi, both using the four headings proposed above, with some additions or modifications.

The relatively simple syllabus presented in Example 6.1 is for a 13-week course with about 30 students.

In the second column (Theory), the professor has recorded the contents and corresponding pedagogical activities. In the third column (Lab), she has indicated the names of the software that the students will use in each lab session. In the fourth column, she has identified the chapters of the textbook that the students are expected to read each week. Finally, in the fifth column, she has indicated the due dates of the assignments (A) as well as the dates of the two tests.

Example 6.1 Syllabus for a Simple Course

Week	Theory (3 hrs/week)	Lab (1 hr/week)	Readings (textbook)	Evaluation
1	• Introduction • Definitions	•Groups •MUSIC	Chap. 1	
2	• Resolution of problems of optimal design, without constraint • Objective function with a single variable, without constraint • Example with GOLD	•BOUND •GOLD	Chap. 2	
3	• General formulation of problems of nonlinear optimal design, with constraints • Example on the board • Directions for A1	•GOLD		
4	• Objective function with several variables, without constraint -criteria of optimality -methods of order 0:3 cases • Formative evaluation • Examples with graphic tool DESMAP	•PS •SPX •PCD	Chap. 3	
5	• Objective function with several variables, without constraint: -methods of order 1 -methods of order 2 • Examples of GBASE and EUREKA	•(continued)	Chap. 3	A1 due
6	• General formulation of problems of nonlinear optimal design, with constraints (continued from week 3) • Directions for A2	•GBASE		
7	• Strategies for solving optimal design problems	•GBASE	Chap. 13	

Example 6.1 Continued

Week	Theory (3 hrs/week)	Lab (1 hr/week)	Readings (textbook)	Evaluation
8	• Solving optimal design problems, with constraints • Linear problems, with constraints • Example on the board	•GBASE	Chap. 4	A2 due
9	• Nonlinear problems, with constraints • Method of direct research • Example with BOX • Directions for A3	•BOX	Chap. 5	
10	• Nonlinear problems, with constraints -criteria of optimality	•BOX	Chap. 5	
11	• Nonlinear problems, with constraints (continued) -criteria of optimality (continued) • Example on the board		Chap. 5	Test (periods 55 and 56)
12	• Methods of transformation from problems with constraints to problems without constraint • Examples with PEN and EUREKA	•PEN	Chap. 6	
13	• Methods of transformation from problems with constraints to problems without constraint (continued) • Summative evaluation of learning	•PEN	Chap. 6	A3
				Final test

The course syllabus presented in Example 6.2 is more complex. It is for a 13-week course taught by 10 professors to 500 students divided into 10 sections — a situation that justifies the details of such a syllabus. The co-ordinator of the course must make sure that all of the professors cover the same content at the same time, do the same activities, and properly use the numerous teaching materials at their disposal.

In the second column, the coordinator has listed the instructional activities; in this course, the students work weekly in groups on projects under the supervision of their section professor. Note how the choice and synchronization of the activities structure the students' work.

In the third column, the coordinator has indicated the approximate time periods allotted for the activities, so that the professors know how much time is available.

In the fourth column are listed the teaching materials needed each week — textbook chapters to read, videos to present and analyze, written materials (CW = materials for class work, GW = materials for group work).

Although this example is long, we present it in its entirety to show how much the serious organization of a course depends on detailed planning.

Example 6.2 Complex Course Syllabus

Week	Activities	Approx. time (min.)	Readings
1	• Introduction of the course • Formation of groups • Exercise: "Meeting the Members of My Group" • Exercise: "The Problem of Leadership in the Group" Video: *Problem of Leadership* • Exercise: "Holding Effective Meetings" Video: *Problems of Holding Meetings* • Full session and instructions by the professor	50 15 15 25 25 20	Course program GW1 GW2 Video RV 081 GW3 Video RV 081 GW4 GW5 (A0) CW3 Chap. 9 and 10
2	• Introduction by the professor • Group meeting -agenda and time frame -reading, approval, and evaluation of report No. 1 -discussion of the content of chapters 9 and 10 -appointment of a leader -distribution of the future reports	5 15	

Example 6.2 Continued

Week	Activities	Approx. time (min.)	Readings
2 (con't.)	• Video: *Engineering Profession* • Presentation by the professor -questions and answers on the special fields -definition of an engineering project and examples of projects -transposition to the mini-project • Brainstorming on mini-project subjects and choice of three subjects to be developed by three students (work due two days later) • Exercise: "Ethical Problems" • Directions by the professor -report No. 1 due -A0 due two days later	25 15 45 25 10	Video RV 055 GW5 (A0) GW6 GW7 GW8 (A0) Chap. 4 and 5
3	• Introduction by the professor -return report No. 1 to the students -confirm the mini-project subject (A0) • Group meeting -agenda and time frame -reading and evaluation of report No. 2 -approval of the mini-project choice by the professor (A0 due) -discussion of the content of chapters 4 and 5 • Full session: clarification and answers to general questions • Group meeting (continued): -work on A1 • Directions by the professor -report No. 2 due	5 30 15 90 10	 GW8 (A1) Chap. 1, 2, 3
4	• Introduction by the professor -return report No. 2 to the students • Group meeting -agenda and time frame	5 135	 GW8

Example 6.2 Continued

Week	Activities	Approx. time (min.)	Readings
4 (con't.)	-reading, approval, and evaluation of report No. 3 -discussion of the content of chapters 1, 2, and 3 -continuation of work on A1 • Directions by the professor -report No. 3 due -A1 due two days later	 10	 Chap. 6 GW9 (A2)
5	• Introduction by the professor - return report No. 3 to the students - feedback on A 1 • Group meeting - agenda and time frame - reading, approval, and evaluation of report No. 4 - discussion of the content of chapter 6 - work on A 2 (beginning) - evaluation of group work - Video: *Problem With a Black Sheep* - first evaluation of the group leader • Directions by the professor - report No. 4 due	10 130 10	GW 9 (A2) GW 10 Video RV 081
6	• Introduction by the professor -return report No. 4 to the students • Group meeting -agenda and time frame -reading, approval, and evaluation of report No. 5 -evaluation of the leader (continued) and appointment of another leader, if necessary -work on A 2 (continuation and completion) • Directions by the professor -report No. 5 due -A 2 due two days later -grade for the leader due	5 15 135 10	GW 9 (A2) Chap. 7 GW 11 (A3)

Example 6.2 Continued

Week	Activities	Approx. time (min.)	Readings
7	• Introduction by the professor -return report No. 5 to the students -feedback on A 2 • Group meeting -agenda and time frame -reading, approval, and evaluation of report No. 6 -discussion of the content of chapter 7 -work on A3 (beginning) • Directions by the professor -report No. 6 due	15 30 95 10	 GW 11 (A3)
8	• Introduction by the professor -return report No. 6 to the students • Group meeting -agenda and time frame -reading, approval, and evaluation of report No. 7 -work on A3 (continuation and completion) • Directions by the professor -report No. 7 due -A3 due two days later	5 135 10	 GW 11 (A3) Chap. 8 GW 12 GW 13 (A4)
9	• Introduction by the professor -return report No. 7 to the students -feedback on A3 • Exercise: "Decision-Making" -Video: *Problem of Decision-Making* • Group meeting - agenda and time frame -reading, approval, and evaluation of report No. 8 -discussion of the content of chapter 8 -work on A 4 (beginning) • Directions by the professor -report No. 8 due	15 25 100 10	 GW 12 Video RV 081 GW 13 (A4)

Example 6.2 Continued

Week	Activities	Approx. time (min.)	Readings
10	• Introduction by the professor -return report No. 8 to the students -explanations for A4, if needed • Group meeting -agenda and time frame -reading, approval, and evaluation of report No. 9 -work on A4 (continuation and completion) • Second evaluation of the leader • Directions by the professor -report No. 9 due -A4 due two days later	10 115 15 10	GW 13 (A4) GW 10 Chap. 11
11	• Introduction by the professor -return report No. 9 to the students -feedback on A 4 -explanations for the final report • Group meeting -agenda and time frame -reading, approval, and evaluation of report No. 10 -division of the work for writing the final report • Evaluation of the teaching • Work on the final report (beginning) • Directions by the professor -report No. 10 due	20 30 15 75 10	CW 13
12	• Introduction by the professor -return report No. 10 to the students -explanations for the final presentation •Group meeting -agenda and time frame -reading, approval, and evaluation of report No. 11 -work on the final report (completion) -preparation of the final presentation • Directions by the professor -report No. 11 due	5 140 5	CW 14 Chap. 12

Example 6.2 Continued

Week	Activities	Approx. time (min.)	Readings
13	• Introduction by the professor -report No. 12 due -return report No. 11 to the students -final report due • presentations by the group representatives to professors from another group (attendance required)	5 145	

The course syllabus, as you can see, provides a synoptic and chronological view of the synchronized activities of a course. Not only does the syllabus serve to guide you through the term, but it can also help when you talk about the course with colleagues or students. That's why we advise you to attach the course syllabus to the course outline that you give your students at the beginning of the term.

6.2 Writing the Course Outline

The course outline is a document of several pages that you give your students during the first class. In it, you explain the structure of the course and summarize the points you covered in preparing your course: objectives, means of evaluation, required texts, and course syllabus. You can even add a section to explain your philosophy for the course or indicate what pedagogical values underlie the conception of the course.

6.2.1 Basic Structure of the Course Outline

In Table 6.2 (on the next page), we propose a basic structure for writing the course outline. It's a structure that you can and should adapt to fit the needs and the pedagogical context of your course. The information usually given in a course outline includes:

- identification of the course and the professor;
- short description of the philosophy of the course (optional);
- course objectives;
- forms of evaluation;
- required texts;
- course syllabus.

Table 6.2 Basic Structure of the Course Outline

<table>
<tr><td rowspan="6">Identification</td><td colspan="4">Identification of the course
• Division and department:
• Term:
• Course number:
• Title:
• Number of credits:
• Time(s) and location(s):</td></tr>
<tr><td colspan="4">Identification of the professor
• Name:
• Office:
• Office hours (days and times):</td></tr>
<tr><td colspan="4">Weekly requirements
• Number of hours of class:
• Number of hours of lab or discussion sessions:
• Number of hours of study at home:</td></tr>
<tr><td colspan="4">Place of this course in the program
• Course prerequisites:
• Concomitant courses:
• Subsequent courses:</td></tr>
<tr><td colspan="4">Course philosophy
• Pedagogical values:
• Requirements for the students:
• Others:</td></tr>
<tr><td colspan="4">Resources and services
• Physical resources:
• Human resources:</td></tr>
<tr><td>Objectives</td><td colspan="4">General objectives:
Specific objectives:</td></tr>
<tr><td>Evaluation</td><td colspan="4">Means:
Weight:
Criteria:
Work due dates:
Name and role of the grader:</td></tr>
<tr><td>Required texts</td><td colspan="4">References:
Cost:</td></tr>
<tr><td>Course syllabus</td><td>Week</td><td>Content and weekly activities</td><td>Students' weekly work</td><td>Evaluation</td></tr>
</table>

Identification. The "identification of the course" part is simple: just provide all of the indicated information.

At the end of a course, it's not unusual to find some students who do not even know the professor's name. Put your first and last names in the course outline, so that students will have at least one document in which your name will be correctly written.

Concerning your availability outside class hours, remember that professors are usually required to hold office hours. So that students can really benefit from this time, you should indicate your days, hours, office number, and telephone number, or tell them how to make an appointment.

For the "weekly requirements" section, you should indicate how many hours per week you expect your students to work and how they are to divide this time: for example, three hours in class, three hours of laboratory or discussion sessions, and three hours of individual study at home.

Since all courses are part of a program, it's useful to indicate to students the "place of this course in the program" by listing the important courses that students take before, during, and after it. You may also want to talk a little about these courses in class, to emphasize what concepts they all have in common.

For courses that use technological materials or special services, you should specify what these services are and where the students can access the physical or human resources at their disposal: computer center, documentation center, special library services, consultation services, etc.

Objectives. With the "general objectives" and "specific objectives" that you list, you can explain what the students will be able to do at the end of the course.

Remember that general objectives are statements expressing the general intentions of the course. They begin, "*Course xxx aims to ... .*"

Specific objectives are statements that detail the general objectives and correspond to the different course themes. Through these objectives, you indicate which cognitive, affective, and psychomotor performances students should achieve at the end of the course, in view of the general objectives. Specific objectives most often begin, "*After studying theme xxx of the course, the student should be able to ... .*"

Evaluation. You then indicate the methods of evaluation — means, types of questions (essay, multiple choice, etc.), dates, and time allotted for the exercises, along with resources permitted, instructions, correction criteria, weighting, and penalties. You may also give the grader's name and specify the role assigned to him or her.

Required Texts. For practically all courses, students must buy one or more textbooks. That's why your course outline should indicate the references and cost for each textbook, and perhaps even where the books can be obtained.

Many professors also provide students with a list of supplementary works to consult. If this list is short (one page or so), you can include it in the course outline; on the other hand, if it consists of several pages, it's better to make a photocopy, to avoid overloading the outline.

Course Syllabus. The course outline should also include the syllabus, so that you can explain to students the activities of the term, session by session.

6.2.2 Example

Example 6.3 illustrates the preceding explanations. Although it's not a universal model for course outlines, it can serve as a guide when you write your own. This example, which uses most of the rubrics from Table 6.2, follows the proposed basic structure.

Example 6.3 Course Outline

COURSE TITLE

DIVISION AND DEPARTMENT

Term

3 credits
(class: 3 hours/week)
(discussion: 2 hours/week)
(work at home: 4 hours/week)

Professor: _____

Office: _____

Office hours: _____

OBJECTIVES

The themes studied in this course are:

- Vector geometry;
- Curves, surfaces, and curvilinear integrals;
- Differentiation;
- Gradient and potential;
- Introduction to linear algebra.

For each of these themes, at the end of the course, the student will be able to:

1. define and explain the concepts;
2. apply the rules and techniques of calculation in routine exercises;

Example 6.3 Course Outline Continued

3. transpose the representations of the concepts, from their algebraic representation to their geometric representation, and vice versa;
4. solve simple engineering problems, in very specific contexts, by appropriately using the concepts and techniques of calculation presented;
5. judge the relevance of the results obtained from the problems and exercises.

Tests 1 and 2 and the final test are required. In the case of a legitimate absence from a test, the grade for this test will be that of the final test.

The tests will focus on evaluating attainment of objectives 2, 3, and 4, and occasionally objectives 1 and 5.

The test dates are indicated in the course syllabus.

The list of test locations will be provided during the term.

EVALUATION

	Weighting	Documentation permitted for the tests*
Test No. 1	30%	1 synthesis sheet
Test No. 2	30%	1 synthesis sheet
Final test	40%	2 synthesis sheets

*For tests 1 and 2, the student may summarize personal notes on an 8 1/2 x 11 sheet, to consult during the test. Two sheets are permitted during the final test.

Lectures
There are three class meetings a week. They require attentive and active attendance.

Discussions
There are two discussion sessions (double periods) a week. The structure of all these sessions, except three, is as follows:

- students work in groups of two or three to solve similar problems;
- students share their solutions;
- a demonstrator provides commentaries or demonstrations.

Example 6.3 Continued

Note: To make these lab sessions more effective — that is, to facilitate interaction between demonstrator and students — these group sessions are small. Since the subgroups do not have the same schedule, which limits the organization of these sessions, the subgroups must remain the same throughout the term.

Self-Tests

The three self-tests are to help the student:

- write a solution;
- verify if he or she has attained objectives 1-5 and modify, if needed, his or her way of studying the problems.

Although these are learning exercises and do not count directly in the calculation of the grade, these self-tests will be corrected.

The student will be able to:

- identify in a solution what is indispensable, important, and what should be written down;
- evaluate the relevance of writing down certain details;
- measure the lack of effectiveness of certain methods.

The students will exchange their self-tests during a discussion session and correct the tests themselves. The demonstrator will propose a solution and its variations and explain the philosophy and the grading scale.

The grade obtained can serve the student as an indicator. It does not reflect the grade he or she would have obtained on a test, but it may allow him or her to identify weaknesses and strengths.

The professor will point out in class the subjects of the assignments and their correction dates.

Required Texts

Primary text:

THOMAS Jr., Georges B., and Ross L. FINNEY. *Calculus and Analytic Geometry*, Part II, 7th ed. Don Mills, Ont.: Addison-Wesley, 1988. $47.85.

Recommended texts:

MORAN, Michel A. *Mathématiques pré-universitaires, fascicule de références*. Montreal: École Polytechnique de Montréal, 1982. $5.00.

WEIR, Maurice D. *Calculus and Analytic Geometry, Student Study Guide*, 7th ed. Don Mills, Ont.: Addison-Wesley, 1988. $16.70.

Example 6.3 Continued

COURSE SYLLABUS

The course syllabus below gives the approximate division of course hours. Under "Readings" are the textbook sections or supplementary texts to read each week. The "Problems" suggested are problems to do at home following the lectures.

This list of problems is not exhaustive; other, more complex problems will be assigned in discussion sessions. To benefit from those sessions, students should have already worked on the problems from the course syllabus.

In addition, the two course texts present, at the end of the chapters, review problems and comprehensive problems. In some cases, there are a lot of problems, so the students should solve a certain number of them, without feeling obliged to limit themselves to the problems suggested.

There are no specific references to the student study guide. However, it's a good idea to study each section of this guide, since each section corresponds to a section of the textbook.

SYLLABUS

Hour	Theme	Work to do at home		Evaluation
		Readings	Problems	
1	Introduction to the course			
2	Vectors in planes and space	sections 13.1 13.2	p. 652, Nos. 27-40 p. 659, Nos. 13-20 and 23	
3	Straight lines and distances	section 13.3	p. 667, Nos. 7, 11, 15, 20, 22, 28, 35, 39	
4	Scalar product	section 13.4	p. 674, Nos. 1, 2, 3, 5, 9, 13, 17, 19, 23, 37	

Example 6.3 Continued

SYLLABUS				
Hour	Theme	Work to do at home		Evaluation
		Readings	Problems	
5	Vector product, matrices, and determinants	section 13.5 13.6	p. 681, Nos. 11, 17, 21, 25 p. 691, Nos. 3, 7, 17, 25, 31	
6	Conics	section 14.1	p. 702, Nos. 1, 3, 5, 13, 17, 19, 23	
7	Translations and rotations of axes	section 14.2	p. 709, Nos. 1, 7, 11, 15, 19, 27	
8-9	Functions, graphs, and level sets	section 14.3	p. 718, Nos. 3, 7, 15, 23, 15, 31	
10	Quadrics	section 14.4 and appendix	p. 728, Nos. 1-16 (name only), 26	
11	Polar, cylindrical, and spherical coordinates	section 14.5	p. 734, Nos. 1, 7, 15, 23, 29, 33, 57	
12	Parametric representation of curves in plane and space	section 14.6, pp. 735-737	p. 743, Nos. 1, 3, 5, 47a), 49	
13	Derivative of a path	section 14.6, pp. 737-742	p. 743, Nos. 13, 15, 19, 35, 39	
14	Length of a curve	section 14.7, pp. 745-746	p. 752, Nos. 1, 3	

Example 6.3 Continued

SYLLABUS				
Hour	**Theme**	**Work to do at home**		**Evaluation**
		Readings	**Problems**	
15	Curvilinear integral of a scalar field		p. 895, Nos. 29, 31, 33	
16-17	Curvilinear integral of a vector field	section 18.1	p. 894, Nos. 1, 11, 13, 21, 23, 26, 27	
18	Introduction to partial derivatives	section 15.1, pp. 765-769	p. 773, Nos. 1, 3, 11, 13, 19, 21, 31, 33, 35, 47, 69	Test No. 1 (material from hours 1-14)
19-20	Linear and differential approximation	section 15.2	p. 778, Nos. 1, 5, 9, 17, 27	
21-22	Composition of functions and concatenation rules	section 15.3	p. 783, Nos. 1, 3, 11, 15 p. 794, Nos. 39, 45, 63	
23-24	Gradient and directional derivation	section 16.1	p. 804, Nos. 1, 5, 15, 21, 23, 29, 31, 33, 37	
25	Gradient, level set, and tangent plane	section 16.2, pp. 805-809	p. 811, Nos. 1, 5, 11, 17, 21	
26	Gradient and implicit differentiation	section 16.2, pp. 809-811	p. 812, Nos. 25, 27, 31, 35, 39	
27	Curvilinear integral of a gradient	section 18.2, pp. 895-898	p. 900, Nos. 1, 3, 5, 9	

Example 6.3 Continued

SYLLABUS				
Hour	**Theme**	**Work to do at home**		**Evaluation**
		Readings	**Problems**	
28-29	Existence and search for a potential	section 18.2, pp. 898-900 section 18.3, pp. 901-903	p. 901, Nos. 17, 18, 23, 27, 29, 33 p. 907, Nos. 5, 7, 11 p. 901, Nos. 17, 18, 23, 27, 29, 33 p. 907, Nos. 5, 7, 11	
30	Generalities on vector spaces	chapter 1	Nos. 1, 4, 11	
31	Linear applications, definitions, properties, and matrices	sections 2.1, 2.2, 2.3	section 2, No. 1 section 3, Nos. 1-3	
32	Operations on linear applications	section 2.4	Nos. 3, 5	
33	Kernels and images	section 2.5	Nos. 1, 3, 4	Test No. 2 (material from hours 15-26)
34-35	Regular and inverse applications	section 2.6	Nos. 1, 2, 3, 4, 6, 8	
36	Base change	chapter 3	section 1, No. 1 section 2, Nos. 1, 5	

Example 6.3 Continued

SYLLABUS				
Hour	**Theme**	**Work to do at home**		**Evaluation**
		Readings	**Problems**	
37-39	Diagonalization	chapter 4	section 1, Nos. 1, 2, 4, 6, 7a), 7c), 7e) section 2, Nos. 2a), 2c), 5, 7	
				Final test (cumulative)

6.3 Preparing Lesson Plans

All professors who have carefully prepared lesson plans affirm that they save an enormous amount of time when you teach a course again, because you have a written record of everything you have done. You only have to review your plans, which makes the time and effort spent preparing them worthwhile.

6.3.1 Basic Structure of a Lesson Plan

The *lesson plan* is an instrument that professors use to detail the content of each class hour. In this document, you specify:

- the subjects to cover;
- the time allotted for your presentations and examples, for each of the subjects covered;
- the materials you will use to illustrate your explanations;
- what you will have to do before and after class;
- what the students will have to do before and after class;
- possible changes to make the next time.

A lesson plan is *short*, usually one or two concise pages. Lesson plans for a three-credit course can form a document of 20-50 pages, depending on your format.

Rather than prepare each class hour separately, you should work in weekly blocks of two, three, or four hours, depending on the circumstances, because that gives you a more global view of the coverage of the subject.

In Table 6.3, we present a basic structure of a lesson plan, that you can adapt to your needs. This basic structure includes the following information:

- identification of the session and its length;
- subjects to cover;
- specific objectives;
- teaching material to use;
- synoptic table clearly presenting the time to allot to each subject and the materials needed to present these subjects;
- things for you and your students to do after class;
- notes about later modifications or improvements.

Identification of the Session and Length. Numbering each week and each class hour facilitates location and identification. We recommend decimal numbering, which allows an unequivocal identification: for example, the numbers 8.1, 8.2, and 8.3 identify three consecutive hours of the eighth week.

The length of a class period varies according to the institution (50, 60, or 75 minutes). If you are working alone, you do not need to indicate the length. On the other hand, if you are coordinating the work of one or more colleagues who are teaching the same course simultaneously using your plans, you should indicate for them the total length of each session.

Subjects to Cover. List the subjects to be treated, following the course syllabus, as well as any reminders, examples, and feedback for an assignment or a test.

Specific Objectives. As we mentioned in Chapter 2, the specific objectives, which clarify the general objectives, are formulated from the student's point of view. Always beginning with an action verb, they complete, in the framework of the preparation for each class period, the following sentence: "*At the end of this period, each student should be able to....*"

Is there any advantage to writing specific objectives when the lesson plan lists the subjects to cover? Definitely. A subject may be associated with different specific objectives. For example, just the mention of the subject

Table 6.3 Basic Structure of the Lesson Plan

Identification of the session and length
Subjects to cover
Specific objectives At the end of this period, each student should be able to:
Teaching materials

Synoptic table

Length	Content	Materials

To do after class

Professor	Students

Comments

"three-phase circuits" does not indicate whether, at the end of the period, the students will be able to:

- *define* a three-phase circuit;
- *distinguish* a three-phase circuit from a single-phase circuit;

- *test* a three-phase circuit;
- *understand* a three-phase circuit;
- *choose* between a three-phase circuit and a single-phase circuit for a given situation.

The advantage of including specific objectives in the lesson plan is that they allow concrete identification of the cognitive behaviors expected of the students for each subject listed. Each of these specific objectives can then constitute a component of the evaluation.

The number of specific objectives for each class period will vary. Experience shows that professors can set two to five objectives per period. Remember, however, that the specific objectives are not always attained during class. Usually, the student can attain a specific objective only through additional work — personal study, exercises, lab work, complementary readings, reflection, or synthesis.

Teaching Materials. Since each class usually requires different teaching materials, indicate what you will use for each period: transparencies (numbered), computer projection system, photocopies, slides, etc.

Synoptic Table. The synoptic table allows you to summarize at least three of the above pieces of information: length, subjects, and teaching materials. You can include more information, if need be.

Under "Length," you note the time to allot for presenting each part of the content.

Under "Content," you simply put what you have already listed in the course syllabus.

Under "Materials," you specify which teaching materials you plan to use: number of a transparency, title of a video tape, title of supplementary photocopies, and so forth.

Completing a synoptic table may require you to readjust your course syllabus somewhat if the time allotments in the lesson plan differ from those in the syllabus. It's better and easier to do this on paper before class than in class as you teach.

Things to Do After Class. Since each course generates a multitude of tasks, for you as well as for the students, make a note of them so that you don't forget any.

For you, the list may include: corrections, looking up information to answer a question, problems to review, room reservation, or preparing instructions for an assignment.

For the students, the list may include: answers to write out after reading a chapter, assignments to hand in, problems to solve, software to consult, or a progress report to prepare.

If you have carefully listed these things to do, you will not forget them or forget to mention them at the end of class.

Comments. After each class, you should note any important details from the experience, things that may be useful the next time you teach the course. These comments may include: changes in time allotments, successful examples, a useful analogy for teaching a given concept, etc. At the end of the term, you can read these comments and consider modifying your lesson plans.

6.3.2 Example

Example 6.4 shows a lesson plan following our recommendations.

This lesson plan for three periods is divided into two parts: hour 2.1, prepared separately, and hours 2.2 and 2.3, using a single plan.

Example 6.4 Lesson Plan

Session 2.1: 50 minutes
Subjects • Review of week 1. • Calculation of the response of a circuit for a given excitation (exercises 1.2, 1.3, 1.4). • Topological definitions of an electrical circuit.
Specific objectives • Calculate the response (voltage, current, power, and energy) of a circuit for a given excitation (voltage source or current). • Define the terms node, branch, loop, and closed circuit in an electrical network.
Teaching materials • Transparency 9: exercise 1.2 (figure 1.14) • Transparency 10: exercise 1.3 (figure 1.16) • Transparency 11: exercise 1.4 (figure 1.17) • Transparency 12: topological definitions of an electrical circuit (figure 2.1)

Example 6.4 Continued

Synoptic table: session 2.1

Length	Subject	Materials	
		Handout	**Transparency**
5	Review of week 1: summary table of chapter 1	-	-
35	Exercises 1.2, 1.3, 1.4	- - -	9 10 11
10	Topological definitions of an electrical circuit	2.1	12

Sessions 2.2 and 2.3: 2 x 50 minutes

Subjects
- Kirchhoff's voltage law.
- Kirchhoff's current law.
- Voltage divider technique.
- Current divider technique.
- Thévenin's theorem (beginning).

Specific objectives
- Explain Kirchhoff's two laws and apply them to a given circuit.
- Use the voltage and current divider techniques to analyze circuits.
- Explain the steps for determining the Thévenin equivalent for a given circuit.
- Analyze time-domain circuits and solve related problems.

Teaching materials
- Transparency 13: Kirchhoff's voltage law (figures 2.3 and 2.4)
- Transparency 14: Kirchhoff's current law (figures 2.5 and 2.6)
- Transparency 15: voltage divider (figure 2.7)
- Transparency 16: current divider (figure 2.8)
- Transparency 17: Thévenin circuit equivalent (figure 3.1)

Example 6.4 Continued

Synoptic table: sessions 2.2 and 2.3

		Materials	
Length	Subject	**Handout**	**Transparency**
35	Kirchhoff's voltage law	2.2	13
35	Kirchhoff's current law	2.3	14
10	Voltage divider technique	2.4	15
10	Current divider technique	2.5	16
10	Thévenin's theorem (beginning)	3.1	17

To do after class
Professor:
- Prepare for the next period.
- Read the class outline for week 3.
- Read the handout (sections 3.1-3.5 and 5.1-5.5).
- Solve the problems from chapter 1 in the collection of problems.

Students:
- Read the handout (sections 2.2-2.5, including example 3.1).
- Do the problems from chapter 1 in the collection of problems.

Comments
- Students tend to confuse the topological definitions of a circuit; emphasize them more the next time; use *all* of the definitions from the handout.
- Transparency 14: corrections to make in the notation.

6.4 Preparing for the First Class

The first class is so important that you should devote 30-60 minutes — depending on the material, the circumstances, and your personality — to attaining the four objectives presented in Section 6.4.2.

6.4.1 Dynamics of the First Class

You never get a second chance to make a first impression.

This same truism applies to your first contact with your students. You leave your students with certain impressions of you and your course; these first impressions tend to last.

In addition, based on these first impressions, each student decides (often unconsciously) whether or not to get involved in the course or to interact with you. These first impressions also form a perspective through which he or she will interpret everything you say and do.

From the start, then, you must establish your credibility with the students, who must notice your enthusiasm for the material and accept your authority and competence.

To do this, you must not try to come across as "the tough guy," "the buddy," "the boss," "the understanding type," or whatever. You must be real, and you must try to meet the basic expectations of the students, for whom your course is a new experience.

6.4.2 Objectives for the First Class

In the first class, you must be interesting and treat your material with enthusiasm, clearly explaining the organization of the course. You must also establish your competence, while working to show your respect for your students and create a favorable climate for work and communication.

To do this, you must try to attain the following objectives during the first class:

- explain the organization of the course;
- gather information about the students;
- arouse interest in the course material;
- create a favorable climate for positive interpersonal relations.

Explain the Organization of the Course. To present the organization of the course, you have the *class outline,* in which you have included all of the important facts — objectives, content, evaluation, specific requirements, texts, course syllabus, etc.

By presenting your course outline interactively that is, by answering questions — you have a good chance of attaining this first objective.

Gather Information About the Students. This information can include their academic profile, the state of their knowledge, and their motivations.

If you have a small class, you can simply ask each student for his or her name and department or division, as well as any courses he or she has taken related to the course material. In addition, a simple discussion will allow students to express their expectations for the course.

If you have a lot of students, you cannot do this orally. To obtain the academic background of each student, you must, for example, ask them to write out the appropriate information on an index card or a sheet of paper.

To ascertain what your students know, you can prepare a diagnostic pre-test focusing on knowledge prerequisite to the course. They can take the pre-test to take at home or in class. This pre-test allows each student to identify his or her strengths and weaknesses before beginning the course. It also allows you to adapt your explanations to the average level of knowledge in your class.

It's more difficult to identify your students' motivations. To break the ice in this area, you can try some group activity techniques.

You might ask the students to write out, taking one minute at the most, a completion to the following sentence: "While coming to this course today, I said to myself ... ." You can then conduct a discussion that should create a certain solidarity among the students by revealing their expectations or motivations. Finally, through the spirit that you infuse into the discussion, you will set a certain climate for your course.

You can obtain the same results by asking the students to gather into groups of four or five to share their expectations, fears, or motivations concerning the course. Afterwards, one student can report the results for each group. The following discussion can then produce the same effects as with the technique suggested above.

Arouse Interest in the Course Material. In order to interest the students in the course material, you must not let your first class overwhelm them. Remember that students like to hear about the relationship between the material and your profession. They appreciate examples and anecdotes. They like to know about your professional activities. They are interested in areas of your research that apply the major theoretical lines of the course. The students must also be made aware of the importance of the course material and of more advanced study of the subject. Only by showing enthusiasm will you be able to reach this third objective.

Create a Favorable Climate for Positive Interpersonal Relations. If all of the steps proposed above take place in a spirit of mutual respect — if you impose only reasonable requirements that your students willingly accept — you can create a favorable climate for work and communication.

6.4.3 Example

In Example 6.5, we offer the scenario of the first class in a course focusing on plastics with about 50 students.

Example 6.5 Scenario of the First Class

Objectives	Activities
• Make informal contact with the students	• Arrive five minutes before class begins and visit with the students as they arrive.
• Become acquainted with the group (5 minutes)	• Introduce myself. Write on the board: last name, first name, office, telephone number, office hours. Also write out the lesson plan for the period. • Describe my training and professional experience in the field. • Talk about my research interests directly associated to the course content. • Talk about the research group that we just formed, to underscore the multidisciplinary nature of the field. • Talk about my pedagogical values and describe my requirements and expectations for the group.
• Gather information on the students (10 minutes)	• Have the students complete the following sentence: "Coming to this class today, I said to myself ... ." Give them one minute and go immediately to a full group session. • Bring out, among their impressions, those that agree and those that do not agree with the objectives and organization of the course. • Once the ice is broken, ask a series of questions to identify the background of the students, their degree of familiarity with the field of plastics, the number of students who want to study in the field, etc. • Evaluate what they learned in courses X and Y the two preceding terms (four fundamental concepts they need to understand).

Example 6.5 Continued

Objectives	Activities
• Show the importance of plastics in daily life and, consequently, the importance of the course (5 minutes)	• In the full group session, ask students to identify, in the classroom, objects made from plastic (floor, chairs, fluorescent tubes, pencils, watches, briefcases, electrical wire, etc.). If time and circumstances permit, repeat the exercise for cars, kitchens, etc.
• Present the pedagogical organization of the course (25-30 minutes)	• Cover the course outline and comment on each of the divisions. Invite students to ask questions, which should be easier for them now that the ice is broken.

The scenario presented in Example 6.5 should help you attain the four objectives for the first class. Note that, in this particular case, the professor chose to make contact with the students, create a climate, and interest them in the field *before* presenting the organization of the course. Also, since the professor is very comfortable with a large group, she conducts all of her introductory activities with the whole class instead of breaking the class into smaller groups.

In preparing for the first class, you should adapt the advice presented here, because no one magic method or activity guarantees that you will attain the four objectives we propose. Whatever you do to prepare for the first class, you should *not simply improvise*, given the important influence of that first impression on the rest of the term.

Review

Course Syllabus

- The course syllabus is a planning tool that allows you to record and synchronize the contents and instructional activities of the course.
- The classic headings of the course syllabus can be presented in the form of the basic structure below.

Course Syllabus			
Week	Weekly content and activities	Students' weekly work	Evaluation

- You should adapt this basic structure to your needs, adding other headings, such as time allotments, discussions, etc.
- It's usually necessary to draft several versions in order to arrive at a satisfactory course syllabus.
- The course syllabus is usually included in the course outline that you give to your students during the first class.

Course Outline

The course outline identifies:

- course and professor,
- objectives,
- forms of evaluation,
- required materials, and
- course syllabus.

Sometimes the course outline also includes several paragraphs in which you present and explain the pedagogical values underlying the course.

Lesson Plan

- The lesson plan is an instrument that allows you to set up chronologically a detailed list of contents and activities for each class period.
- The lesson plan, which you should adapt to your needs, usually includes the following headings:
  - identification of the session,

- length of the session,
- subjects to cover,
- specific objectives for the students,
- instructional materials,
- synoptic table,
- list of things to do after the session, and
- possible notes on improving the course.

Objectives for the First Class

- Explain the pedagogical organization of the course;
- Gather information on the students;
- Arouse interest in the course content;
- Create a favorable climate for positive interpersonal relations.

CHAPTER 7

PREPARING AND DELIVERING A LECTURE

In this chapter, we concentrate on the most widespread teaching method, the lecture, offering some practical advice on how to prepare and give good explanations during a lecture. (As noted earlier, the terms "explanation" and "explaining" come from George Brown, *Lecturing and Explaining* (p. 7): "Put simply, explaining is giving understanding to someone else.")

First, we clarify what we mean by "good explanations." Then we suggest steps for preparing a quality explanation.

Next, we present a general model for lectures based on the procedure recommended here for preparing explanations.

Finally, we propose some communication skills to help you make your explanations more dynamic and interesting.

7.1 Steps in Preparing a Good Explanation

At the heart of the concept of a lecture lies the idea of explanation. *The qualities of a good explanation* are universally recognized:

- it is clear, well-structured, and meaningful to the students;
- it is supported by appropriate examples and accompanied by well-conceived and effective illustrations;
- it intellectually stimulates the students.

More schematically, we can say that in a good explanation you should:

- clearly situate each subject within a conceptual context before explaining it;
- clarify the nature of your explanation;
- clearly bring out the important ideas;
- accompany your explanation with appropriate examples;
- use appropriate teaching materials;
- verify comprehension from time to time.

To prepare explanations that conform to these aims, you can follow a seven-step systematic procedure:

1. List the *subjects* to cover in each period.
2. Use *questions* to identify the *nature* of each subject.
3. Formulate a short, complete *answer* to each question.
4. Find *examples* for each explanation.
5. Identify appropriate teaching *materials*.

6. Devise a way to *verify understanding.*
7. Prepare an "advance organizer." (This expression is proposed by David Ausubel in *The Psychology of Meaningful Verbal Learning,* in the bibliography.)

We will now explain in detail these seven steps and illustrate them with concrete examples.

7.1.1 Listing the Subjects to Cover in Each Period

Before preparing explanations, you must determine your focus. To do so, you establish the *subjects* to cover in *each class period,* which you have already listed in your lesson plan (Chapter 6).

In Example 7.1, we present a list of subjects for the fifth hour of a computer science class in which Turbo-Pascal is taught.

Example 7.1 List of subjects to cover

Use of certain types of data in Turbo-Pascal	
1. The 5 integer types (30 minutes)	2. The 5 real types (30 minutes)
1.1 *Integer* type	2.1 *Real* type
1.2 *LongInt* type	2.2 *Single* type
1.3 *Byte* type	2.3 *Double type*
1.4 *ShortInt* type	2.4 *Extended* type
1.5 *Word* type	2.5 *Comp* type

From a list of subjects like this you prepare your explanations, following the steps that we will continue to detail here.

7.1.2 Using Questions to Identify the Nature of Each Subject

After listing the subjects to cover, you must determine the *nature* of the explanations you plan to give for each of the listed points.

It's important that, from the beginning of an explanation, the students clearly understand the nature of the theoretical development you are undertaking, because this initial identification will orient their coding of the information. If they misunderstand the nature of an explanation, they may subsequently become lost.

Thus, in order for the students to clearly understand the nature of an explanation, you must first clarify it for yourself.

To do this, we suggest a proven method: use questions and answers to clarify the nature of the explanations for each topic and subtopic. We prefer this method particularly because it's easy, since it's based on three categories of well-known interrogative expressions that you use with each topic and subtopic to form questions. With these interrogatives, you can determine whether the nature of your explanations is to *present, describe,* or *justify* (Table 7.1).

Table 7.1 Three categories of interrogative expressions allowing clarification of the nature of the explanations

Category	Interrogative Words
Presentation of facts	*What ...* (To, of, etc.) *what ...* (To, of, etc.) *which ...*
Description of facts	*Where ...* *When ...* *How ...*
Justification of facts	*Why ...*

At this stage in preparing explanations, you clarify *through questions* what you intend to explain concerning each subject listed in the preceding step.

You may merely wish to present or describe a subject or present and justify it. Moreover, you don't need to present, explain, and justify all of the subjects: the verbs you've used in formulating your specific objectives (Chapter 6) indicate whether to present and/or describe and/or justify.

In Example 7.2, we present some questions for explaining the five integer types in the Turbo-Pascal course — questions that begin with one of the interrogative expressions listed in Table 7.1.

The *answers* to these questions will constitute the basic points of the explanations. In the next step, you try to provide a brief but complete answer to each of the questions you have formulated, which allows you to give a clear explanation of each subject.

Example 7.2 Questions for a 30-minute session in a Turbo-Pascal course

Subject	Questions
The five integer types	• **What** are the five integer types? • **What** are the characteristics of each of the five types? • **How** is each of the five integer types used in Turbo-Pascal programming? • **Why** are several integer types used in Turbo-Pascal programming?

7.1.3 Formulating a Short, Complete Answer for Each Question

For students to easily retain an explanation, it must be short and complete. A sentence of two or three lines with a subject, a verb, and an object form a clear, explicit, and unambiguous statement that any student can easily memorize.

These explanations/answers to questions are the core concepts of more detailed explanations that will follow. They are also statements that you will have to prove through subsequent explanations.

At intervals throughout your lecture, you will announce your questions. You will first provide short and explicit answers, giving the essentials of your subject. Then you will provide the full explanations.

In a one-hour session, you can answer a varied number of questions. In certain cases, a single question and a single answer can take the entire class period; most often, however, the explanations needed to cover one or more topics depend on several question-answer pairs.

In Example 7.3, we present for different subject areas a few question/answer pairs that lead into explanations.

Example 7.3 Subjects and corresponding question-answer pairs

Subjects	Questions	Answers
Differential equation	**What** is a differential equation?	• A differential equation is an equation that links an unknown function to at least one of its derivatives.
	What is the order of a differential equation?	• The order of a differential equation is the order of the greatest of its derivatives.

Example 7.3 Continued

Subjects	Questions	Answers
Differential equation (cont'd.)	**What** is a linear differential equation?	• A linear differential equation is a linear combination of the successive derivatives of the function.
	How do we solve a differential equation?	• A differential equation is solved through the following system: $y = ce^{-ax}$ and $y' + ay = 0$
Resistance of materials	**What** information does the tensile strength provide the engineer?	• Through standard tests, the engineer can compare two different materials and define the maximum load to which each can be subjected.
	How can we quickly find the value of the limit of elasticity on a curve of uniaxial stress?	• The value of the limit of elasticity is situated in the zone of the discontinuity curve that corresponds to the beginning of the nonelastic performance of the material.
	Why is it necessary to know the elongation rupture?	• The elongation at the rupture allows us to determine the maximal deformation that a material can sustain without breaking.
Routh criterion	**What** is the Routh test?	• The Routh test is a test to determine the number of poles of a transfer function located at a right angle to the complex plane.
	From **what** information can we verify this test?	• Only knowledge of the characteristic equation of the transfer function is required.
	Why is a Routh test used?	• This test allows us to determine whether an invariant linear system is stable or not.

Example 7.3 Continued

Subjects	Questions	Answers
Types of technical drawings	**What** is a technical drawing?	• A technical drawing is a drawing that presents the three projections of an object: the plane, the elevation, and the profile.
	What types of surfaces do we find in a three-dimensional drawing?	• The surfaces represented in a triple-dimensional drawing can be flat, sloping, or oblique; they can even be curved, in rare cases.
	What is an isometric drawing?	• An isometric drawing is the three-dimensional representation of an object, constructed from three projections.
Measure of the power of three-phase motors	**What** is three-phase power?	• Three-phase power is the total power in phase A, phase B, and phase C, for the motor, generator, transformer, and the transmission line. The following expression is used: $P_T = P_A + P_B + P_C$
	How is three-phase power measured?	• For a circuit without a neutral wire, the sum of the values given by the three watt-meters gives the total power of the three-phase circuit.
	Why is three-phase power measured?	• We measure the power in three-phase because it is the total power used by the machine, industry, etc.

7.1.4 Finding Examples for Each Explanation

After briefly answering the questions you have formulated, you must add detail to the explanations. This means, among other things, finding *one or more examples* to illustrate your answers and help the students better understand them.

You can decide whether to include an example with each answer to a question or wait until the end of the explanations for several question-answer pairs to provide more appropriate examples. We suggest resisting the temptation to always provide just one example, the one that works perfectly. You should use several divergent examples, counter-examples, or a series of progressive examples (from easiest to most difficult, for instance).

7.1.5 Identifying Appropriate Teaching Materials

Next, you must choose the teaching materials to support your explanations: scripto-visual materials, audio-visuals, written materials, computers, or simply voice and gestures (Chapter 5).

7.1.6 Devising a Way to Verify Comprehension

To ensure that the students understand the explanations, you must also consider verifying their comprehension from time to time.

There are several ways to do this:

- Simply ask them questions.
- Do an application exercise on the board, asking them to provide suggestions.
- Pause in your lecture to have students work in pairs for several minutes to solve a problem. You should then reassemble the students, so that you can settle any difficulties that might remain.
- Encourage discussions or debates — as a class or in small groups — when the subjects are appropriate.

In brief, whatever means you choose, you must never continue your explanations without verifying the students' comprehension.

7.1.7 Preparing an "Advance Organizer"

It is to David Ausubel that we owe the idea of the "advance organizer." An advance organizer has the following characteristics:

- It is presented, as a starter, *before* the explanations;
- It contains only general ideas, grouped into a whole;
- It allows the professor to emphasize the *relations* or logical connections among general ideas;
- It must be able to *influence the coding* of information by students.

An advance organizer is a way you can put the subjects of your explanations into a more general conceptual framework. You can provide, in advance, a *structured overview* of the major conceptual directions involved in your explanations and the *relations* that exist among them.

An advance organizer helps prepare the students' brains to code the information to come. It provides a basic structure, a matrix, a framework, an organization (general concepts and relations among these concepts) that they will use to classify and organize the information presented in the explanations.

An advance organizer can be graphic, verbal, or otherwise, and it can use analogies, metaphors, and examples. However, an advance organizer is not the *outline* of a lecture, because this outline, which you put on the board, is only a chronological list of general and specific subjects.

Let's take, for example, the course in Turbo-Pascal used in Examples 7.1 and 7.2. In the partial list of subjects cited, we recorded two types of data: integer types and real types. These are not the only types of data in Turbo-Pascal. The professor could perhaps help students understand the material by presenting, before moving on to integer types, the general context in which these integer types are situated. We would then have an advance organizer similar to the one presented in Example 7.4.

The advance organizer in Example 7.4 allows students to quickly understand that:

- in Turbo-Pascal language, there are four major families of data types: simple, constructed, file, and pointer;
- each of these families is subdivided into one or more branches: simple types are thus divided into scalar types and non-scalar types, and so forth;
- scalar types can in turn be subdivided into other types: integer and Boolean, and so on.

You can also use an advance organizer to help students understand globally, in advance, the organization of the concepts for an entire three-credit course.

At the beginning of a computer-aided design course, a professor used the advance organizer in Example 7.5 to help his students understand the differences that exist between computer-aided layout (CAL), computer-aided design (CAD), and computer-aided manufacture (CAM). In addition, he could show them the computer progression from idea to object: creation of a geometric model, mechanical analysis of the geometric model, and so forth.

Example 7.4 Advance organizer used before studying a new theme

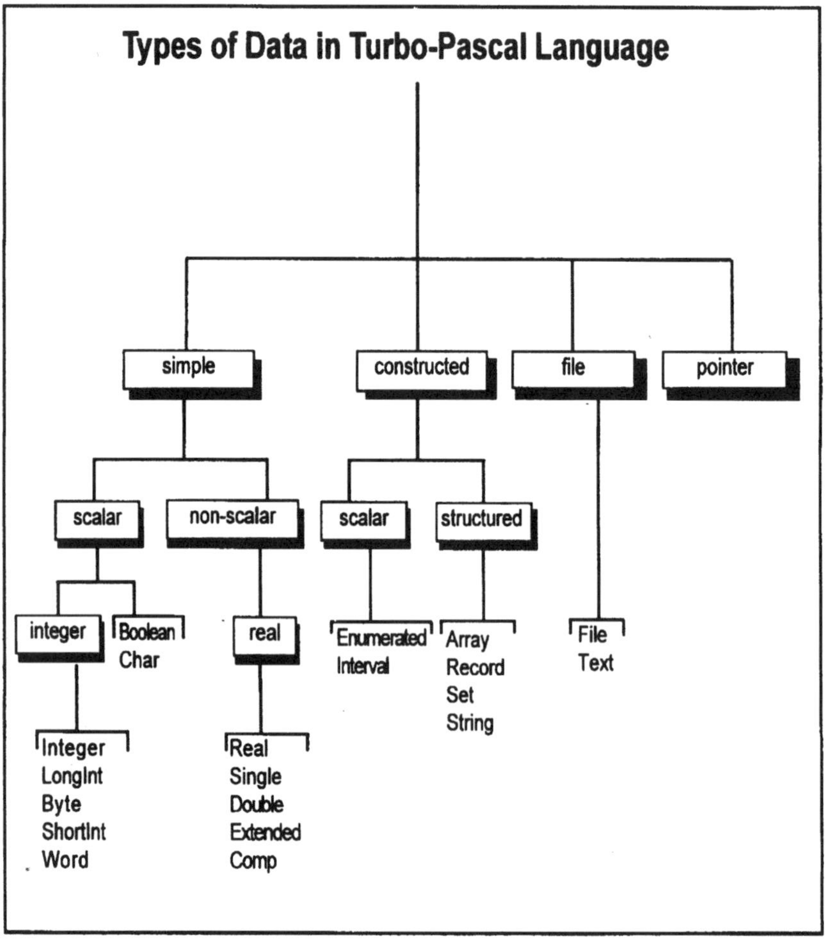

In fact, you can use an advance organizer to introduce a subject as well as to introduce a theme or an important unit of explanations. That's why the number of necessary advance organizers varies greatly according to the course.

A macro advance organizer used at the beginning of a 45-hour course can be followed by as many micro advance organizers as there are themes (units, divisions, parts, etc.) in the course. According to the circumstances, the lectures treating these themes can necessitate other, more specific advance organizers for more limited units of explanations.

Whatever the case, when you use an advance organizer, it must:

- propose a structure or a *general organization* of concepts;
- effectively *influence the coding* of the information in the cognitive structure of the students;
- precede a group of explanations and be presented again regularly, so that students focus on the general structures and not numerous details on numerous subjects.

According to Ausubel, there are two types of advance organizers: presentation and comparison.

Presentation Advance Organizer. This type of advance organizer is used when the material is entirely new to the students. Examples 7.4 and 7.5 illustrate this type. A presentation advance organizer often has the appearance of a *tree*, an *algorithm*, a *block diagram*, or a *conceptual network*. It presents only general ideas and their relations, without details.

Comparison Advance Organizer. This type of advance organizer is used when the domain treated is to some degree structurally similar to a domain with which the students are familiar. A comparison advance organizer is based essentially on the principle of analogies, using a structure that the students already know to help them understand a new structure. The professor uses this analogy like a temporary scaffolding, useful while constructing an explanation, but unnecessary once the students have understood.

Thus, a professor who teaches a course on plastics to students who have already taken a course on metals can refer to the structure for metallic materials that the students already know. They then have a greater chance of understanding — and more quickly — the new characteristics, properties, or performances of plastics, since these aspects are associated with a pre-existing cognitive structure. For example, a brief initial presentation by the professor or a discussion with students at the beginning of a course, using a comparative table, a conceptual network, or a matrix comparing plastics and metals, can help underscore similarities and differences — atomic structures, properties, performances, manufacturing methods, selection criteria, etc. Such activities would constitute comparison advance organizers that can effectively influence the students' coding of the subsequent information.

7.2 A General Model for Lectures

Having prepared the explanations, you need only apply this preparation to the lectures. A clear, structured, and captivating lecture should be similar to the general model we now present.

Example 7.5 Advance Organizer used at the beginning of a 3-credit course

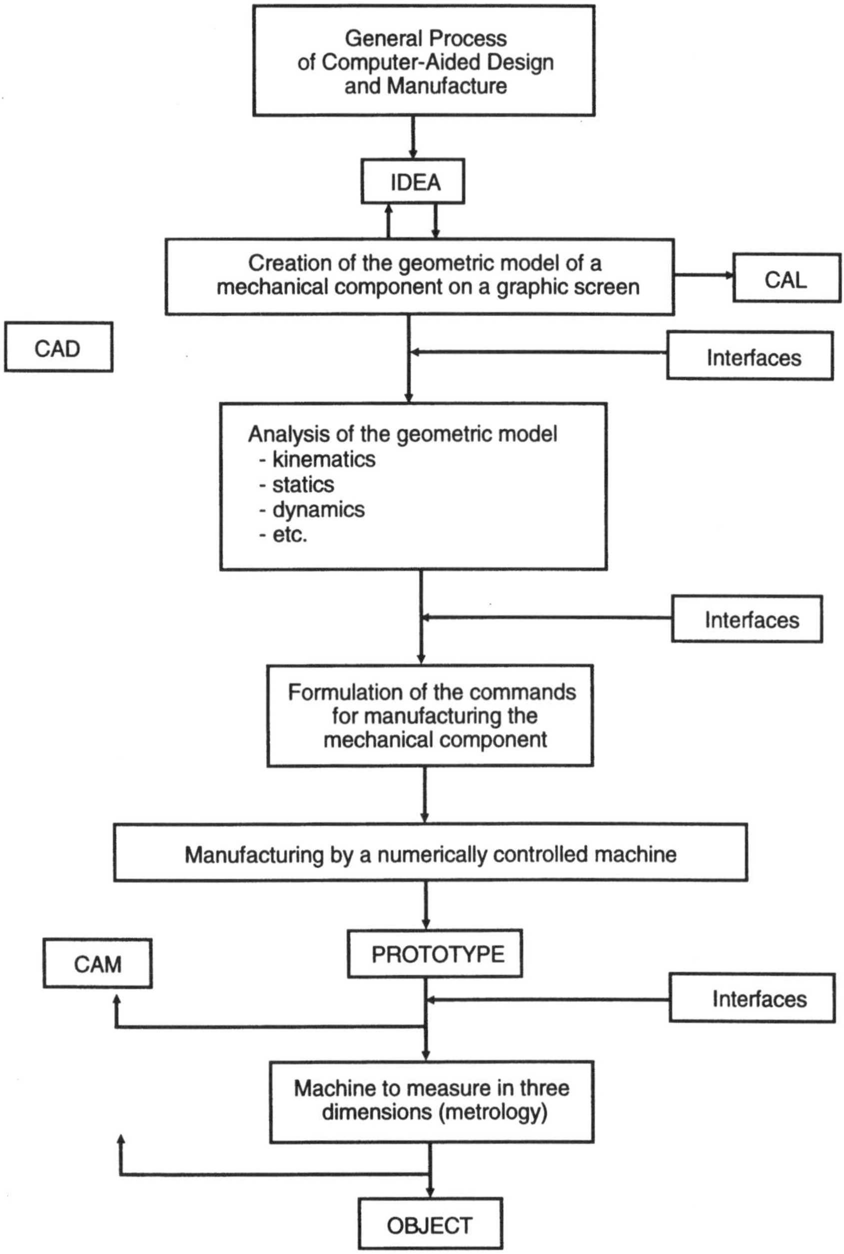

7.2.1 Presentation of the Model

The general model for lectures that we propose in Figure 7.1 conforms to what we just said about preparing an explanation; it repeats, in a certain order, the same steps and elements.

This model is *general*, in our opinion, because it can be used for all subjects, at all academic levels, for all types of explanations. However, this model being — as are all models — an idealization, you cannot hope to apply it point by point; you should adapt it to your specific needs.

This general lecture model is divided into three major parts: a central part, called "explanations," containing the essential; an initial part, "before the explanations"; and a final part, "after the explanations," in which the important activities of the opening and closing of a lecture are listed.

7.2.2 Central Part: "Explanations"

In the central part of the model are the actual explanations. To make sure your students understand, you need to orchestrate a whole series of operations to influence their cognitive structure:

- Present an advance organizer before entering into a new subject;
- State and display, one by one, the question-answer pairs;
- Detail each question-answer pair;
- Give examples;
- Illustrate with the appropriate materials;
- Verify the students' comprehension;
- Repeat each question-answer pair;
- Make a transition and refer to the outline.

Present an Advance Organizer Before Entering Into a New Subject. To provide a clear, structured, and effective explanation, you must first use an advance organizer. It will help you create a general structure to which you and your students can attach the details of subsequent explanations.

State and Display, One by One, the Question-Answer Pairs. Then you state your first question, provide the corresponding answer, and display it (on the board or elsewhere). Each question-answer pair allows you to underscore, from the very beginning of an explanation, the nature of the explanation (presentation, explanation, or justification, Table 7.1). Each question-answer pair brings out an essential idea, conclusion, or principle. The answers must be short (two to three lines), explicit, and unambiguous — each one summarizing in a single sentence (subject, verb, and object) the essence of what you have tried to show.

Figure 7.1 General Model for Lectures

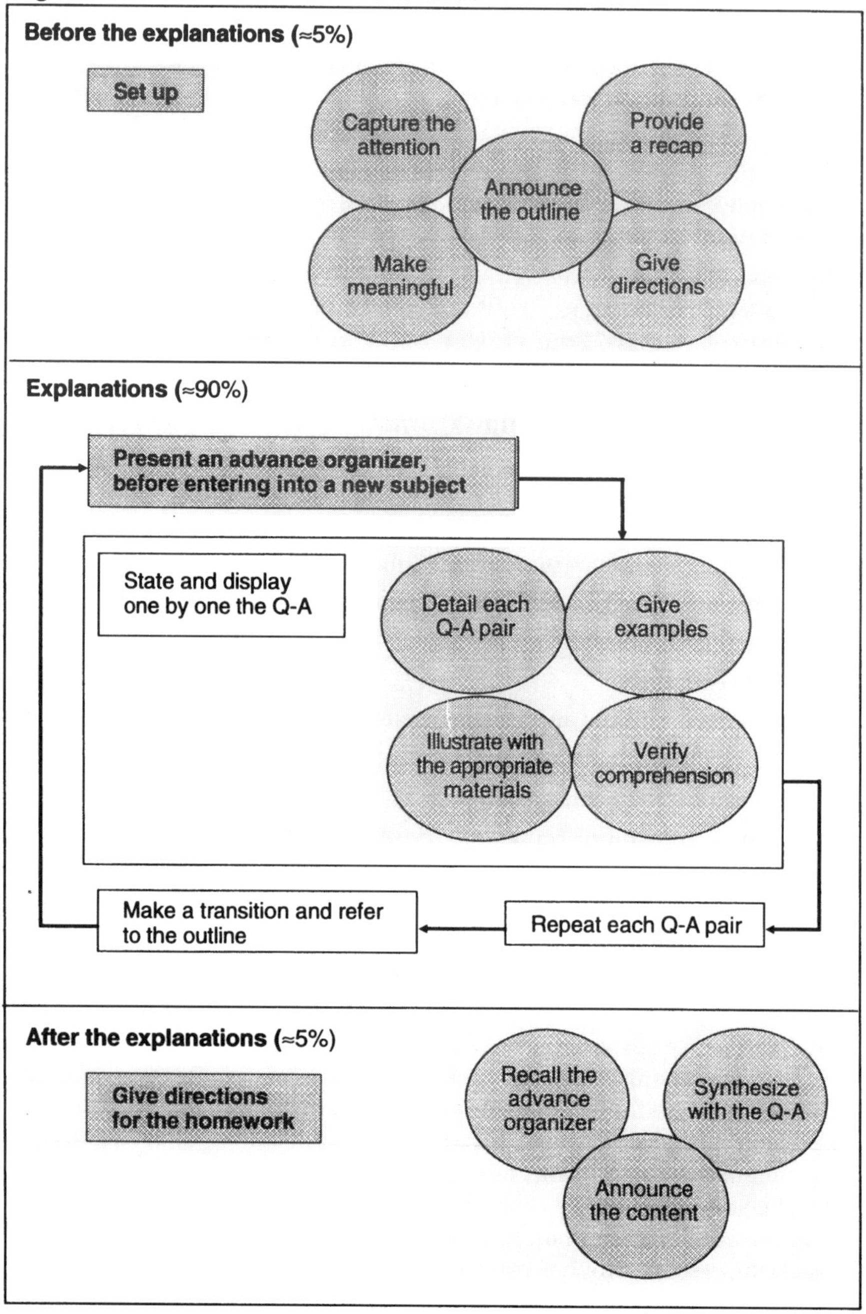

You must give the question and the answer orally before displaying the answer. That allows students to copy it more easily; in addition, youcan emphasize the important words, define new words, announce how you will do your demonstration, etc.

Detail Each Question-Answer Pair. The answer you display often has little meaning for the students who hear and see it for the first time. However, they remember it during your explanation and, gradually, the meaning builds and becomes clear in their minds as you detail your answer.

Give Examples. To help the students understand your explanations even better, you add the examples you have prepared, either for each question-answer pair or for a group of explanations (several question-answer pairs).

Illustrate With the Appropriate Materials. To appropriately illustrate your subject, you can use all of the teaching materials at your disposal that you have planned to use (Section 7.1.5), including your voice, gestures, and expressions.

Verify the Students' Comprehension. To verify how the students have decoded your explanations, you can ask them questions, solve a problem on the board with them, have them do exercises in groups of two, or begin a discussion.

Repeat Each Question-Answer Pair. When, at the end of your explanation, you repeat the answer you gave at the beginning, the students are in general satisfied that they have understood, which constitutes a positive reinforcement — a reinforcement that will encourage them to try harder to understand the next explanation.

Make a Transition and Refer to the Outline. When you have completed this cycle for a question-answer pair, you can refer again to the outline you presented at the beginning of the class to situate your explanation, make the transition between one explanation and the next, and start the cycle again with a new question-answer pair.

7.2.3 Initial Part: "Before the Explanations"

We will now examine what you should do before the explanations themselves — that is, what constitutes the introduction to your lecture:

- Set up;
- Capture the students' attention;
- Provide a recap;
- Announce the lecture outline;

- Make the lecture meaningful to the students;
- Give the students useful directions so they follow the class.

You must do all of this (Figure 7.1) in a relatively short time. Your introduction should not take more than 5% of the total time of the lecture — about three minutes for a 60-minute session.

Set Up. Before presenting the introduction for your lecture, you must set up comfortably in order to be able to talk without discomfort, effectively, without wasting time and without having to constantly look for your materials during the time that follows.

To do this, arrive in class several minutes in advance. This allows you to:

- put your notes appropriately on the board,
- verify the order of transparencies or slides,
- focus the projector,
- return papers or distribute photocopies to the students,
- write the lesson plan on the board,
- answer questions your students might have, and
- talk with students.

Capture the Students' Attention. To capture the students' attention at the beginning of class, you should prepare, for each introduction, a different and unpredictable opener, such as:

- a fact or statistic drawn from current events and linked to the subject to be covered,
- a quote,
- an object,
- an anecdote,
- a caricature,
- a question asked of the students, or
- a recent event, linked to the course, that has impressed the students.

The purpose of this opener is to quickly stimulate the students on the sensory and intellectual levels: first, by capturing their physical, visual, and auditory attention; then, by directing their cognitive attention to the subject(s) to be covered.

Provide a Recap. Once you have captured the students' attention, you can recall what you presented previously to establish continuity with what you plan to cover in your lecture.

This way, you help the students restore in their short-term memory the information, procedures, and postulates that will help them work together for the class period. Through a review, you activate the students' memory and intellectual faculties, which will facilitate their coding of new information.

In addition to this first kind of recap, you must also remind the students of the work that they've done since the last session — readings, exercises, assignments, research, etc.

You can identify what the students have retained and understood and, if you find that they've experienced certain difficulties, you can briefly return to the explanations relating to the misunderstood points.

This way, you also show the students that you care about what they do between classes, and you clearly demonstrate your interest in their progress — which is quite likely to encourage them to put a regular and sustained effort into studying the material.

Announce the Lecture Outline. Since a good lecture is well-structured, you must show your organization by announcing your lecture outline before beginning the explanations.

You can do so orally, although that demands that students listen carefully and remember well. You can also write it in brief on the board or display it in detail on a transparency. The former allows the students to refer to the outline throughout the entire period. The latter means that the outline may not remain in view, as you will probably show other transparencies. You can remedy that disadvantage, however, by keeping this transparency at hand in order to show it again at the right moment.

You can also follow the course outline that you gave to the students or use the table of contents of a handout or textbook as your outline.

With the lecture outline, the students always know where they are; they can follow your lecture better and take more organized notes by referring back to the appropriate headings and subheadings.

Make the Lecture Meaningful to the Students. For students to understand, learn, retain, and transfer new information to another situation, they must find meaning in it, because no information is meaningful in itself. A piece of information has meaning when taken in context with other information or, in the framework of a course, when you show its importance and use in the professional world.

Therefore, you must make new subjects meaningful. To do so, you can:

- refer to the specific objectives you want the students to attain, allowing you to explain how acquisition of these new subjects will be useful;

- demonstrate that professionals regularly use the material these subjects cover;
- link these new subjects to theoretical developments you presented earlier, to show how they proceed logically;
- show that the new subjects are at the foundation of other subjects that you will present later;
- prove to the students that understanding a new subject will allow them to accomplish, for example, part of a class project, or a laboratory assignment.

The care you take to justify the importance of acquiring a new subject can be a determining influence on your students' learning. Very often, it can make the difference, in the students' eyes, between banal learning, which they may quickly forget, and significant learning, which will encourage them to be more attentive and more willingly do the subsequent intellectual work.

Give Useful Directions. At the beginning of a class, you can sometimes give students certain directions that will help them take best advantage of your lecture. Tell them whether or not they need to take notes, which pages in the textbook are pertinent, when is the best moment to ask questions, whether they need to sign an attendance sheet, or whether you're circulating some object or showing a video document, etc.

7.2.4 Final Part: "After the Explanations"

We will now discuss what you should do after the explanations — that is, what forms the conclusion of the lecture. You should:

- recall the advance organizer;
- synthesize, using the question-answer pairs;
- announce the content of the next class;
- give directions for the homework.

These actions "after the explanations" (Figure 7.1) should take only a relatively short time. The length of the conclusion is the same as that of the introduction, about 5% of the total length of the lecture. Three minutes is reasonable for a 60-minute session.

However, the conclusion should not be too short: 30 seconds, in the last minute of class, while students are organizing their belongings, is inacceptable pedagogically. If you want your students to benefit from your conclusion, you must prepare it carefully and not deliver it too quickly.

Most professors neglect, it seems, to anticipate conclusions to their lectures, so they regularly fail to provide them. This phenomenon is so widespread that students are surprised when a professor takes the time, at the end of a class, to review the points covered during a session. Nevertheless, the conclusion is important pedagogically, as we will demonstrate.

Recall the Advance Organizer. You should return, after the explanations, to the advance organizer provided at the beginning of class.

The fact that you use the same advance organizer at the end of your lecture helps students understand the concepts presented and their relationships much better than in the introduction.

Also, if you were unable to cover all of the subjects planned or show all the relationships among these subjects, the students can use the advance organizer to evaluate the area covered and what remains to be covered. Finally, by returning to the advance organizer, you reinforce the global and synthetic view, helping the students step back from the often analytical aspect of the explanations.

Synthesize With the Question-Answer Pairs. In your conclusion, it's wise to reconsider and regroup the question-answer pairs you prepared and presented one by one during the lecture; this allows the students to verify their understanding of the essential points of your presentation. By repeating the main ideas, you appeal to the students' long-term memory, by proposing a new perspective of these essential ideas — a perspective that only the retrospective of the conclusion allows them to appreciate.

In practical terms, you can, for example, copy these question-answer pairs on a transparency or on photocopies to distribute to the students. If you provided course note handouts, the conclusion of each chapter could include these question-answer pairs.

Announce the Content of the Next Class. You should always briefly announce, at the end of a lecture, the content of the next session, to give students an idea of the continuity of the different sessions of the course. This announcement will also reinforce the structure of the class for the students and possibly even whet their appetites for the subjects to come.

Give Directions for the Homework. Finally, at the end of a lecture, you should always specify the work to be done for the next class or provide a reminder: readings, exercises, due dates, subjects to review for a test, etc. To keep these directions short and clear, it's better to write them out or include them in the course syllabus for the students (Chapter 6).

7.3 Some Communication Skills

To intellectually stimulate your students, you must not only provide them with clear, well-structured explanations, but you also must be as dynamic as possible. To do this, you should master the elementary pedagogical communication skills that we present below.

7.3.1 Varying Your Voice, Gestures, Movements, and Eye Contact

To capture and hold the students' attention during class, you must present lectures that stimulate, because even a well-prepared explanation can be boring. You do not need to put on a show and become an actor; you only have to vary your voice, gestures, movements, and expressions, which allows you to project your presence.

Voice. You should be careful with your volume, your pronunciation and articulation, your intonations, and your delivery.

Your *volume* is appropriate when you speak loudly enough so that all students hear you. You should avoid giving the impression that you are sharing secrets, but you need not bark as if you were giving orders. Ideally, especially in a classroom, you should project your voice slightly and keep it lively by varying your volume — for example, to emphasize certain parts of your explanations: transition, important points, or conclusion.

If you teach a large class in a large room, you should use a microphone, for two reasons: so that students hear you perfectly and so that you can speak comfortably, without losing your voice. Whatever your situation — amphitheater or seminar — you should always ask your students if they can hear you well. They will tell you, because their comfort depends on it. They will also appreciate your respect for their needs.

You should take care with your *pronunciation* and *articulation* as well. Speak clearly but without affectation, pronounce each word without mumbling, and don't let your voice fade as you end your sentences.

In addition, you should vary your *intonation* to give color and texture to your speech. You can present certain explanations in a positive and assured tone, state a problem in an interrogative or doubtful tone, or provide the solution for it by adopting an enthusiastic tone. You can even skillfully use silences or "micropauses" to emphasize an idea or give it time to enter the students' mind.

Finally, you should adjust your *delivery* so that you don't bore or exhaust your students. Be neither too slow nor too fast. And don't attemp to present volumes of material in a short period of time. In the latter case, you should, in preparing, adapt the content to the time allotted.

Gestures and Movements. You must appropriate your teaching space by using proper gestures and movements. Do not limit your territory to just the podium or your desk; extend it to include the entire classroom.

As you lecture, you should avoid remaining seated or immobile near the overhead projector or the board. You should move around — at opportune moments, of course. You can move to point out a word on the board or to give students the time to read or copy a sentence. You can also move among the desks or tables to affirm your presence, to encourage the students to participate more actively in a discussion, and so forth.

Appropriate gestures and movements, associated with varied inflections of your voice and variations of your expression, will allow you to capture and hold the often fleeting attention of your students.

Eye Contact. You must also learn to emphasize your explanations with your eye contact. To do this, you must first acquire the habit of looking at your students. *Look at one person at a time,* for a certain time, and periodically change your "target," to have at least visual contact with each student during class. You can also read their faces for indications of understanding, incredulity, or concern.

7.3.2 Asking Questions

Most professors ask their students relatively few questions during class. According to recent research on postsecondary teaching, professors devote barely 3% of their time in class questioning their students. In addition, 63% of this 3% is spent on questions that are vague and not intellectually stimulating, such as, "Is that clear?" "OK?" "Has everyone understood?" "Does anyone have a question?"

It takes more than vague questions to verify that students are understanding a lecture. You should plan your questions and their degree of difficulty. Certain questions require students to recall facts. Others verify their understanding or their ability to use the new information. Still others force them to demonstrate their analytical skills, their sense of synthesis, or their critical judgment.

7.3.3 Answering Questions

When students ask questions of you, you can answer them appropriately by proceeding in three stages:

1. Reformulate the question.
2. Answer the question directly, straightforwardly, concisely, and precisely.
3. Verify that your answer is satisfactory.

Reformulating a question offers two advantages: first, you make sure you have understood the question; second, you ensure that all the students have heard it. That way, you will answer the question and not miss the point, and the students will not have to listen to an inappropriate "answer." In addition, by addressing the question to everyone, you can hope that a greater number of students will participate in the answer or in any resulting discussion.

After answering the question, you should instinctively verify that your answer satisfies the student who asked the question. To do so, simply ask, "Have I answered your question properly?" or "Is that answer all right?" or use a non-verbal equivalent (nod your head, etc.).

Review

Steps in Preparing a Good Explanation

1. *List the subjects* to cover in each class period.
    - This list must correspond to the content list in the course syllabus.
2. Identify, in *question* form, the *nature* of each subject.
    - Using three types of interrogatives, write questions that allow you to clarify the nature of the subjects:
        - presentation of facts: *who, what, which;*
        - description of facts: *where, when, how;*
        - justification of facts: *why.*
3. Formulate a *short, complete answer* to each of the questions.
    - Answer in two or three lines the questions formulated in step 2.
    - Each answer must include a subject, a verb, and an object.
    - Each answer must be unambiguous.
4. Find *examples* for each explanation.
    - Use examples frequently.
    - Use more than one example, including counter-examples.
    - Do not hesitate to use several examples of increasing complexity, one after the other.
5. Identify appropriate teaching *materials*:
    - written materials;
    - visual materials;
    - audio-visual materials;
    - computer programs;
    - your voice, gestures, and eye contact.
6. Devise a means of *verifying* the students' *comprehension.*
    - You can:
        - ask the students questions,
        - do exercises on the board involving the students;,
        - have the students do exercises in pairs,
        - initiate a discussion or debate (entire class or small groups).

7. Prepare an *advance organizer*:
   - presentation advance organizers;
   - comparison advance organizers.

Some Communication Skills

- Vary your voice by paying attention to:
  - volume,
  - pronunciation,
  - articulation,
  - delivery, and
  - intonation.
- Vary your gestures and movements by:
  - not remaining seated;
  - not remaining immobile in the same spot;
  - moving about among the desks or tables;
  - putting words on the board or an overhead projector;
  - being expressive (hand and arm movements, facial expressions, etc.).
- Vary your eye contact by:
  - looking at one student at a time;
  - periodically changing your "target."
- Ask students questions:
  - formulate questions that call on all of the taxonomic levels of cognitive objectives (memorization, comprehension, application, analysis, synthesis) and apply the students' critical sense;
  - avoid such stock questions as "Is that clear?" "OK?" "Do you have any questions?"
- Answer questions by:
  - reformulating them;
  - being concise and precise;
  - verifying that the answer is satisfactory.

CHAPTER 8

TRAINING STUDENTS FOR GROUP WORK

In this chapter, we propose a strategy for training students in group work. We do so because most students have never learned the elementary rules underlying effective group work — simply because no one has ever taught them those rules!

However, since group work is standard in modern professional life, professors absolutely must prepare their students for this kind of activity. In addition, through group work, students develop professional skills that a lecture course would not even allow them to imagine. They develop:

- their ability to share leadership in a group;
- their sense of organization, belonging to a group, and sharing tasks;
- their ability to hold effective meetings;
- their sense of responsibility, autonomy, and initiative.

In Section 8.5 of this chapter, we propose a training strategy for group work to help students consciously develop the skills listed above.

However, given that this strategy is based on a body of knowledge that many professors do not possess, we devote Sections 8.1, 8.2, 8.3, and 8.4, respectively, to the study of:

- the distribution of energy in good work groups;
- recommendations for the first sessions of work for a group;
- recommendations for effective participation of group members;
- characteristics of an effective meeting.

You will have to transmit this knowledge to your students, of course, because this transfer is one of the elements of the training strategy proposed in Section 8.5.

8.1 Distribution of Energy in a Good Work Group

A good work group is a group whose members know how to make judicious use of the total available energy of the group. In other words, the team must be able to transform the latent energy of each member into group energy.

Two factors allow this transformation of individual energies into group energy: identification and validation of a common goal and creation of harmonious interpersonal relations.

According to psychologist Yves Saint-Arnaud (*Les Petits groupes — Participation et communication*, Montréal: Presses de l'Université de Montréal, Éditions du CIM, 1978), the total energy available in a group (E_t) is divided into productive energy (E_p), solidarity energy (E_s), maintenance energy (E_m), and residual energy (E_r). Therfore:

$$E_t = E_p + E_s + E_m + E_r$$

We will study in greater detail each of these four types of energy that constitute the total available energy necessary for a group to function well.

Productive Energy. In a good work group, most of the total available energy must be dedicated to production — that is, to attaining a common goal or achieving the assigned task.

In a group, productive energy is strong when the members have a clear and common view of the task to be accomplished. The less ambiguous their perception is of the task, the more the members unanimously value the attainment of the common goal, and the stronger the productive energy of the group.

However, the productive energy is effective only to the extent that certain obstacles do not momentarily conflict with the use of that energy. As we will see later, if there are obstacles, the team must consume a certain amount of maintenance energy to overcome them.

Solidarity Energy. A certain part of the total energy in a work group must be used to create and maintain solidarity — that is, to establish harmonious, strong, durable interpersonal relations, based on confidence.

Without solidarity, the team risks having production difficulties. The amount of energy needed to create solidarity is greater than initially believed; however, a group should expend less solidarity energy than productive energy.

Solidarity energy in a group is strong when the members are able to show each other friendship, understanding, and respect, in spite of differences in personality or expressed viewpoints.

Solidarity energy, moreover, is all the stronger to the extent that the group members enjoy meeting, discussing, and establishing favorable interpersonal relations in the framework of attaining a shared goal. Such a work climate breeds the assurance and confidence that make the use of production energy more effective.

Conversely, a group in which solidarity energy is weak risks working in a tense climate, with mind games and individual frustrations that undermine the appropriate use of productive energy. The group must then use a greater amount of maintenance energy than normal to establish a favorable work climate.

Maintenance Energy. A certain part of the total energy in a good work group must be devoted, as necessary, to maintaining favorable work conditions. In fact, in spite of functioning harmoniously, sometimes a group is confronted by obstacles that can undermine progress as well as the work climate. In such cases, the team must be able to transform part of its total energy into maintenance energy to overcome these obstacles.

Indeed, a good work group is *not* necessarily a team that is never confronted by obstacles. Rather, it's a group whose members are able to alleviate or dispel the effects of obstacles that undermine pursuit of the common goal or the creation and maintenance of harmonious interpersonal relations.

However, there's a risk of suffocation when a team spends too much of its total energy on maintenance. Although maintenance is essential, it must not be the primary goal of the work group. The primary goal is to complete a task in the best possible conditions.

Residual Energy. In a good work group, residual energy must be minimal, because it's individual energy that is not transformed or invested in the group — in short, it is *unused* energy. Members who refuse to become involved, who are absent, who arrive late without a valid reason, who remain indifferent to everything, who are quiet during meetings, who hide their discontent or any other feeling, and so forth — these members generate residual energy.

When the amount of residual energy in a group is greater than the sum of all the other energies, that group has little chance of accomplishing its task. Conversely, the lower the residual energy, the greater the chances for success.

In *summary*, members of a good work group are able to:

- identify and value the pursuit of a common goal,
- create and maintain harmonious interpersonal relations,
- overcome obstacles that hinder productive activities, and
- become involved on all levels.

8.2 Recommendations for the First Sessions of Group Work

When you create work groups in class, you must understand that each group is, in the beginning, only a simple gathering of individuals. It does not truly exist as a productive and living entity; rather it is a "group in the making."

That is why the members of each group must use, in their initial meetings, part of the total energy of the group to do the following:

- Establish a good relationship;
- Compare their individual perceptions of the shared goal;
- Define and distribute the tasks necessary to get the work done;
- Make sure that each member expresses himself or herself and gets involved.

These actions all help the group transform individual energies into group energy. The group can use this energy to attain the two principal objectives of a good group:

- to identify and set a high value on a shared goal;
- to create and maintain harmonious interpersonal relations.

Establish a Good Relationship. Sometimes, the first contact among the members of a group can be limited to simple introductions and an exchange of addresses, telephone numbers, times available, etc. Other times, the members want to get to know each other a little better. So a discussion starts that allows all of them to talk about the resources they think they bring to the group, their requirements for group work, and what they think about the task assigned to the group.

Compare Individual Perceptions of the Shared Goal. When the group is formed, it's important to make sure that each member is trying to attain the same group goal. Most people involved in group work consider this verification a waste of time, because they're convinced that the other members share the same perception of their goal. However, experience often proves the contrary: individual perceptions of the common goal are indeed surprisingly varied.

That's why, in order to avoid wasting productive energy, the group members must compare — from the beginning and, if necessary, as the work progresses — their individual perceptions of the common goal, so that each can make any essential adjustments.

Define and Distribute the Tasks. For a group to function well, it's important that each member's tasks be clearly defined. The members must determine who will lead the work sessions, who will be the secretary or the reporter, and so forth. These roles and the corresponding tasks must be precisely identified and accepted by all the members, which allows them to avoid improvisation and facilitates a coherent and harmonious organization of all the activities.

Make Sure Each Member Gets Involved. So that all the members of the group participate actively in the work, communication must be clear, frank, and open. Then, as we have already mentioned, residual energy will be almost nonexistent. To communicate effectively, however, all group members must be attentive to verbal and nonverbal messages, so that they can identify any problems due to uneasiness, an impression of secrecy, or disagreement. They can then settle problems as quickly as possible.

8.3 Recommendations for Effective Participation in Group Work

Once the members of the group have begun working toward achieving the task at hand, they must be careful to constantly apply certain principles that will allow them to maintain optimal participation and communication. Each member must always make sure to:

- participate sometimes as "transmitter," sometimes as "receiver,"
- address the group and not one single individual,
- participate positively,
- participate in leadership roles,
- show respect for the others, and
- communicate his or her feelings and impressions.

We will now explain in detail each of these recommendations.

Participate Sometimes as "Transmitter," Sometimes as "Receiver." During a group meeting, participation varies constantly. Some people choose an active role as transmitters of messages, while others take a more reserved role as receivers. A few moments later, however, these roles can be reversed. That's normal, since all members of a group cannot play the role of transmitter at the same time.

On the other hand, it's not normal for the same people to be transmitters too often while the others are simply receivers. Indeed, if one member is limited to a single role, it handicaps the group, because productive energy and solidarity energy depend in large measure on how well each member passes from the role of receiver to the role of transmitter, and vice-versa. All of the members must make sure that there is a certain mobility of transmitter and receiver roles in the group.

Address the Group, Not One Individual. When a member speaks, he or she must make sure to address the whole group and not a single member. It often happens that a member of the group may speak to one other member, such as the leader. In such a case, residual energy increases among the members "excluded" from the conversation. In fact, members who address a single person rather than the whole group jeopardize the solidarity and cohesion of the group, consciously or unconsciously, because they fail to use the resources of the neglected members.

By addressing the whole group, each member constantly broadens the field of participation and prevents a few members from monopolizing the discussion.

Participate Positively. Consciously or unconsciously, each group member plays one or more roles, psychologically speaking. Some of these roles exert a positive psychological influence on the productivity and life of the group, while others exert a negative psychological influence.

Positive participation. Some people take advantage of their natural talent as *organizational leaders* or *affective leaders* to positively influence the productivity or affective life of the group. Others are natural *peacemakers,* calming emotions and reducing tensions when things go wrong.

Still others are *facilitators* who know how to curtail digressions by recalling the objective or by encouraging those who wander from the point to keep on track.

Some people tend to be *clarifiers* who are not afraid to ask questions that others might hesitate to ask. Others are *motivators,* skillful at proving to each member that his or her collaboration is invaluable, which contributes to lasting peace.

All of these roles, and many others of the same type, lead to a positive participation — one that contributes to improving the perception and validation of a shared goal, and creates and maintains harmonious interpersonal relations.

Negative participation. Negative roles undermine optimal use of the total energy of the group because they undermine productive energy and solidarity energy. In addition, members who adopt negative roles increase residual energy and diminish maintenance energy.

Among these people are the *criticizers,* who dispute everything said and done in the group, and the *inhibitors,* who slow down the work by constantly taking positions of principle or adopting strict and rigid attitudes. The *pessimists* believe the group will never be able to solve the problems, that it will not have enough time, that the members are incompetent, etc. The *unconcerned* and *silent* members are there, but not heard.

The *pretentious* members overestimate their abilities and often take credit for solutions proposed by others. Finally, the *manipulators* pursue hidden agendas apart from the common objective; they are often flatterers who do not hesitate to use political games, cunning, humor, blackmail, and the like to gain support for their ideas. In addition — and this is why they are harmful to the group — manipulators are often skillful and very intelligent.

It goes without saying that group members should strive for positive participation so that the group attains its goals.

Participate in Leadership Roles. In a good group, effective leadership does not depend on a single individual. It must integrate the diverse influences that all of the members can exert on one another.

We often use the label "born leader" for any person who exerts a strong influence in a group. However, this label encourages the belief that, in a group, leadership is the characteristic of someone stronger, someone superior to the others. We believe, on the contrary, that leadership in a group must be a collective experience.

Consequently, we consider leadership a dynamic in which all of the group members participate. Leadership causes behaviors that create affinities. The "born leader" is only a member whose influence is perhaps greater, in some aspects, than that of the other members of the group.

The leadership assumed by the group members as a whole can be positive or negative, of course — positive if it facilitates optimal group productivity and negative if it undermines it.

Show Respect for Others. Each member of a team must respect the others and recognize the importance of the resources that each person can contribute.

Each group member naturally feels the need to be esteemed and accepted by his or her partners. If this basic need for personal security is not satisfied, the individual will have difficulties participating in the group activities, in actualizing his or her potential, and in communicating confidently.

To show respect and goodwill, a member can welcome the others warmly, inform them of his or her satisfaction with their work, and show interest in their points of view, their emotions, and their feelings.

Communicate His or Her Feelings and Impressions. If certain feelings about the group cause a member to feel less a part of the group, it is his or her duty to tell the others about those feelings. Otherwise, he or she increases the group's residual energy.

In a group that wants to attain a common goal, each member must be able to communicate without fear. It's a normal use of maintenance energy that allows the disaffected member in question to restore his or her solidarity with the group.

8.4 Characteristics of an Effective Meeting

Many professors have noticed that groups of students often hold inadequate meetings. Such meetings inevitably lead to frustration, an impression of wasted time, and, consequently, a decline in commitment to the common task.

That is why, to help students hold effective meetings, we propose that you provide them with information on the three following aspects, which we will analyze in detail:

- how to prepare for a meeting;
- how to conduct a meeting;
- how to close a meeting.

8.4.1 Preparing for a Meeting

Although the need to prepare for a meeting is commonly acknowledged, many students improvise their meetings. Improvisation does not make meetings more effective. Each member must know his or her role perfectly, whether leader, secretary, or participant.

The Leader's Role. The leader plays a major role in preparing for a meeting. The leader must remind the others, each week, of the date and time of the next meeting. He or she must also remind people of the work they must do for that meeting and make sure this work is done on time.

The leader must also check, well before the day of the meeting, that the minutes of the preceding meeting, taken by the secretary, do justice to the remarks and decisions made during that meeting.

In addition, the leader must prepare the agenda for each meeting and anticipate the approximate time to allot to each of the points.

The agenda for group meetings in a course is a very simple document, as the model shown in Example 8.1 indicates.

As we see, the title of the document, "AGENDA," clearly appears at the top of the page, as does the number of the meeting. Different identification elements follow, according to the needs of the group or the requirements of the course:

- designation of the group;
- title of the project;
- title of the course;
- date of the meeting;
- starting and ending times for the meeting;
- meeting place.

The agenda usually includes, before the list of items, the following standard points:

- attendance,
- appointment of the secretary (if need be),
- adoption of the agenda and time frame for each item, and
- reading and approval of the minutes from the preceding meeting.

The list of items then follows, according to the work to be accomplished.

Example 8.1 Agenda for a project meeting in an engineering course

AGENDA **Meeting No. 5**

Group 4, Team H
Project: Thermostat control by telephone
Meeting of Sept. 5, 1994
8:30 to 10:30
Place: A-410

Points on the agenda

1. Attendance, absences, appointment of the secretary, adoption of the agenda and the time frame for each point (5 minutes)
2. Reading and approval of the last meeting's minutes (10 minutes)
3. Critical study of Chapter 7 from the handout, "How to Conduct a Feasibility Study" (15 minutes)
4. Assignment 3: feasibility study (85 minutes)
5. Conclusion
   - summary of the work accomplished
   - distribution of the tasks (5 minutes)
6. Miscellaneous

Patrick C.
Leader

Finally, the agenda often includes a final heading, "miscellaneous," which allows participants to add one or more items when they approve the agenda.

The Secretary's Role. To prepare for a meeting, the secretary must write up the minutes for the preceding meeting. He or she must also present these minutes to the leader at least one day before the meeting date, in case the leader considers it advisable to make changes so that the minutes more acurately reflect the decisions made by the group. Then, the members of the group are more likely to quickly approve the minutes, which saves invaluable time.

The minutes are a short document (two or three pages) that does not follow a specific format. They are often structured according to the items on the agenda and the course of the meeting. They may also include commentaries on participation, difficulties, and so forth.

Example 8.2 presents the minutes for the meeting whose agenda was set in Example 8.1.

Here again, the title, "MINUTES," appears prominently at the top of the page, as well as the number of the meeting.

Different elements of identification follow, as in the agenda:

- name of the group,
- title of the project,
- date of the meeting,
- starting and ending times of the meeting,
- meeting place.

After that, according to custom, attendance is taken and absences and late arrivals are noted. The secretary of the meeting is chosen, as well as the agenda, the time frame for each item, and so forth.

In addition, in one or two short sentences, the minutes reiterate the objective(s) of the meeting and indicate if the agenda of the present meeting is accepted as is and if the minutes of the preceding meeting are approved without change or if there are changes to make.

Finally, the minutes summarize, point by point, the discussions and decisions for each of the items on the agenda — items that serve as the structure for the minutes.

When they serve as secretaries for a meeting, some students are content to report only the basic facts: "The group met; we discussed such and such a point; we made certain decisions and divided the work among the members; etc."

Example 8.2 Minutes of a project meeting in an engineering course

MINUTES FROM MEETING NO. 5

Group 4, Team H

Project: Thermostat control by telephone

Sept. 5, 1994

8:30 to 10:30

Place: A-410

1. Attendance, appointment of the secretary, adoption of the agenda and the time frame for each item

Present:

John A.

Sylvia B.

Patrick C., leader

Dao Kim D., secretary

Absent:

Luke E., excused absence

Late:

Dao Kim D.

The opening of the meeting is delayed for five minutes while we wait for Dao Kim D., who is the secretary for meeting No. 5. Patrick, the leader, reminds us that today we must complete the feasibility study (assignment 3) for our project.

To do this, we must identify, among the solutions listed, those that should be *rejected* and those worth *retaining* for the preliminary study, the object of assignment 4.

The group adopts the five items of the agenda and the time frames proposed by the leader.

John A., the secretary for meeting No. 4, reads the minutes of that meeting. They are approved without change. The group also congratulates John for the clarity of his work.

2. Critical study of chapter 7 from the handout, "How to Conduct a Feasibility Study"

The professor had asked us to think about two questions before reading this chapter:

What are the advantages of a feasibility study for an engineering project?

What difficulties do you anticipate when applying such a study to your mini-project?

Example 8.2 Continued

According to the majority of the group members, the principal advantage of a feasibility study is that it proposes a systematic, but nonetheless objective procedure that allows comparison of an impressive number of solutions.

We anticipate certain difficulties, however, in applying a feasibility study to our mini-project, especially since we will have to estimate costs and calculate time frames.

Since our lack of knowledge and experience does not allow us to make informed judgments on these two aspects, we plan to ask the professor for advice when we arrive at this stage of assignment 3.

3. Completion of assignment 3: feasibility study

Systematic analysis of the six listed solutions using the four criteria — "physical aspects," "economic questions," "time factors," and "environmental factors" — led us to:

reject solutions 1, 2, and 6, and

retain solutions 3, 4, and 5 for the preliminary study (assignment 4).

The justifications of our decisions are appended, as for assignment 3.

4. Conclusion

The leader summarizes the work accomplished and identifies the work remaining to be done by the due date for assignment 3.

It is agreed that Dao Kim D., the secretary of the meeting, will write up the minutes tomorrow. John A. and Sylvia B. will take care of the first draft of assignment 3, which the leader, Patrick C., will review.

The leader suggests a short supplementary meeting to let each member of the group give assignment 3 a final review. This meeting is planned for next Tuesday, Sept. 13, at 1:30. If changes are necessary, there would be one day to make them before handing in assignment 3 to the professor.

Sylvia points out that, for once, the meeting went well, as the team worked seriously and effectively. Congratulations to all! The leader, however, reproaches Dao Kim D. for arriving late. All members understood the message!

The leader decides to inform Luke F. of the work completed today. It is agreed that Luke will have to do extra work on assignment 4 to compensate for his absence today.

The meeting ends at 10:30.

Dao Kim D.

Secretary

Such minutes are useless because they lack details. Although the minutes should be a summary, they must be sufficiently detailed: they should record not only that there were discussions, but also the main lines of these discussions. In addition, the minutes must clearly indicate the nature of the decisions made and identify who is in charge of executing them.

Role of Each of the Members. The nature of the preparation that each member of a group must do before a meeting varies greatly. Members may all have to complete the same task; each may have a specific individual task as well. Whatever the tasks may be, the members must take them seriously. A member must not, for example, decide not to do the common task, counting on the fact that others will do it, because he or she would then generate residual energy. If several members, or all of them, adopt such an attitude, the group will face serious difficulties in its solidarity as well as in its productivity.

8.4.2 Conducting a Meeting

We offer below some recommendations for conducting a meeting, taking for granted that the group has already named, at the beginning of the term, a leader to plan, organize, and conduct each of the meetings. In addition, in this group a different member plays the role of secretary, according to a rotation set at the beginning of the term.

Welcoming the Participants. Before a meeting begins, it's important that the members of the group strengthen the affective links that unite them in order to reactivate production of solidarity energy. This responsibility is not incumbent only upon the leader: each member shares the responsibility. Of course, if a warm welcome does not take place spontaneously, it's up to the leader to be attentive to the group dynamics and to ensure this process of solidarity.

It has been observed that brief affective exchanges at the beginning of a meeting often translate into greater effectiveness, due to the understanding and confidence created or revived among the participants.

Opening the Meeting. When it's time to begin the meeting, work starts even if one of the members is missing. The leader must not wait; he or she must instead respect the punctuality and commitment of the members who have arrived on time by beginning right away — unless those present decide, at the start, to wait for the other, whose presence they judge essential to the meeting. Such a decision would show group initiative, not that the leader is lax or poorly organized.

The Leader's Role. The leader is responsible for opening the meeting. He or she verifies the presence or absence, excused or not, of each member.

He or she has the group accept the agenda and approximate time frames and approve the minutes of the preceding meeting.

From the beginning, the leader makes sure that the objective of the meeting is clear and that all of the members understand it in the same way.

During the meeting, the leader sees to it that each member can freely express his or her ideas and emotions. He or she also makes sure that the group respects the timetable.

The leader can also take the floor to express his or her point of view, being careful not to monopolize the discussion. If confronted by a situation in which his or her roles as moderator and participant conflict, the leader should ask another member to temporarily assume duties as leader.

The Secretary's Role. During the meeting, the secretary records the remarks, discussions, and decisions of the group. From these notes, he or she later writes up the minutes of the meeting.

If the secretary wants to become involved in a discussion, he or she should ask another member to take notes temporarily.

Participants' Roles. We merely reiterate here that, during a meeting, all members who are not serving as leader or secretary must:

- participate positively, so that they don't impede the group's progress;
- make sure that fellow members can assume the roles of transmitter and receiver;
- participate in the leadership;
- show respect for the other members;
- address the group and not one single individual;
- be attentive to verbal and nonverbal affective messages, in order to maintain a climate favorable to productivity.

8.4.3 Closing a Meeting

When a meeting has run well and the group seems to have attained the set objective, the participants should not simply gather their things and prepare to leave without closing the meeting, even if only a few minutes remain.

Hasty departures often bring meetings to an abrupt end. However, a meeting is not over as long as one important step — too often skipped — remains: the conclusion.

The conclusion consists of two steps: summarizing the work accomplished and evaluating how the group has functioned, if need be.

Summarizing the Work Accomplished. Usually, the leader takes charge of summarizing the work accomplished, although the secretary can also assume this task. A summary must be brief, concise, structured, accurate, and objective.

A good summary never lasts more than *five minutes*, because the participants are tired — a final sprint, yes, but not a long-distance run.

A good summary must state the *essentials*, avoiding details and digressions. The members retain a synthesis much better than a presentation that mixes primary and secondary elements.

The summary follows the main lines of the major topics covered, the decisions made, and the order of the discussions. What's important is that the participants clearly perceive the structure of the meeting.

In summarizing, the leader must show *no bias* for one idea or another, presenting the facts without distortion. In addition, he or she must not minimize the importance of conflicts or agreements. The summary should accurately report both the results and, as necessary, the procedures adopted and the emotions of the members.

Indeed, if care is taken in the agendato give a summary and record it in the agenda, there will be no surprises. In addition, the members will become more aware of what took place during the meeting and more accurately remember the results, the conclusions, and the division of the tasks — and this will enhance their impression of working effectively.

Evaluating the Functioning of the Group. To make the most of a meeting, a group can critically and at regular intervals examine how it functions by reviewing four main aspects:

- the flow of the meeting,
- the quality of communication,
- the quality of the participation, and
- the quality of the leadership.

In terms of *flow*:

- Did the members respect the established rules?
- Did the members follow the planned steps?
- Was the procedure coherent?

In terms of *communication*:

- Was the work atmosphere pleasant?
- Were the participants aggressive?

- Was each member able to speak?
- Were there useless repetitions?

In terms of *participation*:

- Did each member have the impression that the others were listening and understanding?
- Did the members feel that everyone was committed to the common objective and involved in pursuing it?
- Did any members unintentionally behave in a way that slowed down the activities or harmed their teammates?

Finally, in terms of *leadership*:

- Did the leader prepare and organize the meeting well?
- Did the way in which the leader conducted the meeting satisfy everyone's expectations?
- Was the leader sufficiently directive?
- Was he or she able to coordinate and structure participation?
- Was he or she able to focus participation as necessary to encourage the group in its pursuit of common objectives?
- Was his or her summary appropriate?

Because the points just considered are very general, they can be analyzed by evaluating several types of meetings. In practice, it's often better to consider only a few of these points at a time or even consider them only at specific turning points in the life of the group. It's a judgment call for students interested in improving their work meetings.

8.5 Proposal for a Training Strategy in Group Work

No universal way exists to train students to work in groups; each professor can proceed as he or she thinks best. Moreover, the form and length of this training often depend on the number of students and certain other circumstances. Nevertheless, we propose here a method that we have tested for several years with thousands of students. It has proven very effective.

8.5.1 Objectives of the Strategy

If you want to train students for group work, we suggest that you achieve these four objectives:

- Make the students aware of the distribution of energy in a good work group.

- Teach the students what they must do to build a group from the first work sessions.
- Teach the students to participate in the group framework to ensure a favorable climate for continuous productivity.
- Teach the students to hold effective, productive, and satisfying meetings.

8.5.2 Term Breakdown of Activities Using the Proposed Strategy

To achieve these objectives, we suggest a training strategy distributed over the entire term, based on three principal types of activities. The students should:

- complete certain exercises during the term,
- read short texts on working in groups and holding effective meetings (or you can give a presentation on these topics), and
- write weekly reports.

This strategy requires a minimum of effort from you; the students do most of the training through the exercises. For the most part, you simply supervise the exercises and read the weekly reports.

Example 8.3 presents activities for group-work training over a 14-week term. We explain these activities in detail, week by week.

Since this is only an outline, you can (and should) adapt this schedule of activities to your specific needs and the time available.

Example 8.3 Activities for group work training in a 14-week term

Weeks	Activities
1st week	**A. Forming groups**
	B. Exercise 1 Students start with an exercise titled "Meeting the Members of My Group." In this exercise, each student introduces himself or herself to his or her teammates; the members then discuss the methods that they want to apply to their group work.
	C. Readings or presentation You then assign the students short readings on *the distribution of energy in a good work group* and *holding effective meetings*. If you cannot provide these texts, you can cover the content in one or two presentations.

Example 8.3 Continued

2nd week	**A. Discussion** After the students read the texts, or after the presentation(s), you ask the groups to compare the conclusions they drew from exercise 1 with the more theoretical information in the texts or the presentation(s).
	B. Exercise 2 The members of each group then *name a leader* and clarify his or her role. Each group also develops a calendar, *including the weekly rotation of secretaries.*
3rd and 4th weeks	**Application** The groups meet each week to work on their projects. Each week, the secretary of each group writes up the minutes of the meeting and submits them to you. You use these minutes to follow the evolution of the work of the groups and to identify the groups that seem to be experiencing difficulties.
5th week	**Exercise 3** You ask the students to do a *first formative evaluation of the strengths and weaknesses of the group.* You then ask them to make concrete suggestions to improve the situation. *You also ask each group to do a first formative evaluation of the leader.* The members can either propose concrete suggestions to improve the situation or, if the situation requires it, change leaders.
6th, 7th, and 8th weeks	**Application** The groups continue to meet each week and submit the minutes of their meetings to you.
9th week	**Exercise 4** You ask the students to do a *second formative evaluation of the leader.*
10th, 11th, 12th, and 13th weeks	**Application** Same as 6th, 7th, and 8th weeks.
14th week	**Exercise 5** You ask each student to do an *individual assessment* of what he or she has learned from the group work. Each student must also make recommendations that will help him or her in subsequent group work, either in another course or in his or her career. This individual assessment (one page) is attached to the report of the meeting of this last week of the term.

8.5.3 Detailed Account of Training Activities for Group Work

8.5.3.1 First Week

A. Forming groups

Following our strategy, groups should be formed in the first week. You must determine:

- the number of students per group;
- whether to draw lots or to let groups form naturally.

Number of students per group. In our opinion, grouping two or three people to accomplish a task does not lead to proper training for group work. For students to really assume the challenges of a true work group, the group should consist of four or five members. In the framework of large-scale projects distributed over two terms and requiring a multidisciplinary approach, groups may consist of seven or eight members — the maximum acceptable in an academic context.

For real training in group work, there must be:

- a leader and a secretary;
- formal meetings consisting of thorough discussions, with each member contributing experience or work;
- communication instruments such as agendas and minutes;
- a somewhat detailed calendar that is planned and followed;
- coordination and distribution of tasks;
- management of complex interpersonal relations and resolution of any conflicts.

It's difficult for groups of two or three members to assume all of the challenges noted above and, consequently, to ensure effective training in group work. Only groups of at least four or five members offer this possibility.

Formation of groups. If your students do not know each other, you can form groups by drawing names at random. All of the groups then have the same number of members and, theoretically, the same abilities.

On the other hand, when the students already know each other, for the most part, and a certain number of them have already worked in a group in other courses, you should respect their natural propensity to want to work together again. However, you must also take into account the students who do not know each other.

In this situation, you should establish a compromise between the desire of students to form the same groups and the pedagogical necessity to encourage them to work with new teammates.

Students who have already worked together can form the same group again, on the condition that they integrate at least two new teammates into this group.

Some groups accept this condition immediately, while others deliberately break up and their members agree to work in entirely new groups. Such groups are more likely to be evenly balanced, with the chances of success better distributed among the groups.

B. Exercise 1: "Meeting the Members of My Group"

Once the groups are formed, their members absolutely must get to know each other, as soon as possible, right from the first week of class. We propose in Example 8.4 a basic exercise to help them get acquainted and promote the production of solidarity energy in each group.

Example 8.4 Exercise 1: "Meeting the Members of My Group"

Objectives	• Identify each member of the team. • Ensure that each member tells his or her partners what he or she brings to the group and offers his or her suggestions for effective meetings.
Time	• About 35 minutes.
Method	• Directions: 1. Name a leader and a secretary. 2. Read all of the directions for the exercise. 3. Carry out the different steps of the exercise.
	STEP 1: Introductions (about 5 minutes) One by one, each member gives his or her full name and telephone number, after repeating the names of those who preceded him or her. The others record the names and numbers of each member on a copy of the list below. Class No.__________ Group No. __________ First name Last name Telephone No. ____________________ ____________________ ____________________ ____________________ ____________________

Example 8.4 Continued

Method	**STEP 2: Experience in group work and requirements** (about 10 minutes) Write out your comments for the following four points: 1. Here is what *I liked* about my last experience with group work. __________ __________ __________
	2. Here is what *I did not like* about my last experience with group work. __________ __________ __________
	3. Since we will be working as a group, *here are my suggestions* for effective meetings. __________ __________ __________
	4. Here are *the qualities that I believe I contribute to the group.* __________ __________ __________
	STEP 3: Discussion (about 20 minutes) The leader first makes sure that each member of the group tells the others what he or she wrote for the four points. Then he or she leads a discussion to reach unanimous agreement on work suggestions. The secretary summarizes this discussion in a report that he or she submits to you.

You can shorten this exercise if time is tight, of course, by deleting one of the points. However, the final discussion must not be eliminated because it is crucial for the group. Of course, if all of the group members know each other, you should adapt this exercise.

C. Readings or lectures: *The distribution of energy in a good work group* and *holding effective meetings*

After Exercise 1, you suggest several readings for the students to do at home, on the distribution of energy in a good work group and holding effective meetings. Ideally, the content of these readings should be related to the content from Sections 8.1, 8.2, 8.3, and 8.4.

Through these readings, students draw from a common source and learn new vocabulary for these two topics. In addition, they can compare the conclusions that they drew from Exercise 1 with the content of these readings.

To do this, they should read the texts with two questions in mind. Both will serve as bases for discussion at the beginning of the second week:

- What differences and similarities have you identified between the conclusions drawn by your group after Exercise 1, "Meeting the Members of My Group," and the content of these readings?
- Do you have additional recommendations to make your group work more effective and more satisfying?

In the bibliography, we suggest some other readings that you can recommend to your students.

If you cannot get these works or the students cannot read them, you can give a lecture on the characteristics of a good work group and on holding effective meetings, using the information presented in Sections 8.1-8.4. In this case, we recommend stressing the following notions:

- the distribution of the total energy in a good work group;
- recommendations for the first work group sessions;
- recommendations for optimal participation by all members;
- the leader's role in preparing, conducting, and closing a meeting;
- the secretary's role during meetings, including the content of the minutes of meetings;
- the role of the other members during meetings.

8.5.3.2 Second Week

A. Discussion

Discussion of the two questions presented at the end of Section 8.5.3.1 should allow the groups either to confirm the conclusions they drew from Exercise 1 or make additional recommendations. In addition, each student can give a more detailed point of view on group work, so that the members get to know each other a little better before choosing a leader and secretaries.

B. Exercise 2: *Naming the leader and secretaries*

In the second week of class, the students choose a leader to serve for the entire term. Since the role of leader is central, it's preferable not to change the leader each week, in order to ensure a certain continuity and stability in the way the group functions and in its productivity.

Leading the group is a very heavy responsibility. To encourage the leader to take that responsibility seriously, we suggest that the other group members evaluate him or her twice during the term — first in the fifth week, then in the ninth week.

In the second week, the group members must identify precisely the criteria by which they will evaluate the leader on these two occasions. Through these criteria, they will be able to offer suggestions for improvement or dismiss the leader if they find him or her totally incompetent.

The role of the meeting secretary should rotate every week among the other members. This sharing of tasks allows each member to become more involved, in order to ensure a pleasant climate and proper functioning of the group.

Each week, the group members evaluate the minutes of the preceding meeting. This evaluation should encourage each secretary to do quality work.

In Example 8.5, we propose a method to guide the students in choosing a leader and secretaries.

Example 8.5 Exercise 2: Naming the leader and secretaries

Objectives	• Name a leader for the entire term. • Establish a calendar setting the rotation of secretaries. • Clarify the tasks of the leader and secretaries.
Time	• About 15 minutes.
Method	**STEP 1: Naming the leader** (about 7-8 minutes) 1. Every member who wants to become leader steps forth as a candidate by stating his or her reasons and how he or she envisions that role. 2. The group votes. 3. Once the leader is elected, the other members specify the responsibilities and the tasks that they confide in him or her to help the group achieve its goal. ***Leader's contract*** Here is the list of tasks and responsibilities entrusted to the leader. He or she will be evaluated twice during the term by the members of the group, using these criteria. ________________________ ________________________

Example 8.5 Continued

Method	STEP 2: Naming the secretaries (about 7 to 8 minutes) Names 2nd week: ________ 3rd week: ________ 4th week: ________ 5th week: ________ 6th week: ________ 7th week: ________ 8th week: ________ 9th week: ________ 10th week: ________ 11th week: ________ 12th week: ________ 13th week: ________ 14th week: ________ ***Secretaries' contract*** Here are our requirements for writing the weekly minutes. Each secretary's minutes will be evaluated weekly using these criteria. ________ ________ ________

8.5.3.3 Third and Fourth Weeks

During the third and fourth weeks of class, you let the groups hold their work meetings as they please. The students work on their project by trying to apply what they have just learned about the characteristics of a good work group and holding effective meetings.

You should require, however, that each group produce a weekly report on its activities. By directly supervising the students in class and reading the minutes of meetings every week, you judge the evolution and quality of work in each group. If a group experiences difficulties, you are quickly aware of them and can offer help.

8.5.3.4 Fifth Week

Exercise 3: ***First formative evaluation of the group and the leader***

In the fifth week, you ask the students to do their first formative evaluation of the strengths and weaknesses of the group and the leader. This first formative evaluation allows the students to invest a certain amount of maintenance energy in the group, and to perhaps benefit from improvements over the next nine weeks.

To evaluate the group, each student reflects on the strengths and weaknesses that he or she has identified in one month of work. He or she then evaluates the aspects of the group that influence productivity and solidarity among the members.

To evaluate the work accomplished by the leader in the beginning of the term, the students must review the list of tasks and responsibilities that they established in Exercise 2 (Example 8.5) and use these criteria to complete the survey that we propose in Step 2 of Exercise 3 (Example 8.6).

All the conclusions drawn from this evaluation are of course recorded in the meeting minutes for the fifth week.

Example 8.6 Exercise 3: First formative evaluation of the group and the leader

Objectives	• Identify the strengths and weaknesses of the group after several weeks of work. • Evaluate the work accomplished by the leader. • Make suggestions to improve the work of the group and the leader.
Time	About 20 minutes.
Method	Directions: 1. The leader directs the exercises while the secretary takes notes. 2. Read all of the exercise instructions. 3. Complete the two steps of the exercise. **STEP 1: Evaluation of group strengths and weaknesses (about 10 min)** In Exercise 1, each group established a list of suggestions for the work to be accomplished. • Reread these suggestions. • *Individually*, identify the strengths and weaknesses that you perceive in your work group. • Share your opinions and discuss them in such a way as to make appropriate recommendations for improving the work of your group. *Strengths of our group work* ____________________ ____________________ ____________________ ____________________

Example 8.6 Continued

<table>
<tr><td>Method</td><td>
Weaknesses of our group work ____________________
____
Recommendations ____________________
____
____

STEP 2: Evaluation of the leader (about 10 minutes)
• Individually, evaluate the leader, in writing, using the survey below.
• Share the results of these evaluations and discuss them in such a way as to make recommendations to the leader. If the evaluations are unanimously very negative, the group should plan to name another leader.

Survey
Indicate, using the scale below, your degree of agreement or disagreement with each statement about your group leader.
1: Completely disagree with the statement
2: Somewhat disagree with the statement
3: Somewhat agree with the statement
4: Completely agree with the statement
1. The leader begins each meeting effectively. ☐
2. The leader clearly recalls the objectives to be attained at each meeting. ☐
3. The leader knows how to encourage each member to participate in the meetings. ☐
4. The leader facilitates communication among group members during meetings. ☐
5. The leader generally succeeds in helping the group attain the objective(s) of each meeting. ☐
6. The leader generally succeeds in following the planned time frame for the different activities of a meeting. ☐
7. The leader knows how to effectively close a meeting (progress of the work, distribution of the tasks, and evaluation of the functioning of the group). ☐

Overall, how would you rate the leader's work? (Check one.)
Excellent ☐
Very good ☐
Acceptable ☐
Poor ☐
Unacceptable ☐
Comments ____________________
____
____
</td></tr>
</table>

Example 8.6 Continued

	STEP 3: Suggestions for the leader ______________________________ ______________________________ ______________________________ ______________________________

8.5.3.5 Sixth, Seventh, and Eighth Weeks

In the sixth, seventh, and eighth weeks, the students continue to work as in the third and fourth weeks under your supervision.

8.5.3.6 Ninth Week

Exercise 4: ***Second formative evaluation of the leader***

In the ninth week, you ask the students to do a second formative evaluation of the leader, applying the same method as in Exercise 3.

If the leader has done good work, this evaluation constitutes a positive reinforcement. If not, it's the final opportunity for him or her to correct any problems.

8.5.3.7 Tenth, Eleventh, Twelfth, and Thirteenth Weeks

From the tenth through the thirteenth week, the students continue to work on their project under your supervision.

8.5.3.8 Fourteenth Week

Exercise 5: ***Individual assessment***

In the last week of class, you ask each student to attach an individual assessment to the last meeting report, stating what he or she learned as a result of the group work.

Although the form of this assessment matters little (see Example 8.7), the student absolutely must make a series of recommendations that could be useful in subsequent group work, in another course or in his or her professional life.

This individual assessment should testify to the quality of each student's awareness, perspective, and thought. This retrospective should also allow the student to adopt more informed behaviors in work groups or meetings in the future.

Example 8.7 Exercise 5: Individual assessment

Objective	• To establish an assessment of what you have learned about the principles governing group work and holding effective meetings.
Number of pages	One.
Method	• Review the texts concerning the distribution of energy in a good work group and holding effective meetings. or • Reread the notes you took during the professor's lecture on the characteristics of a good work group and holding effective meetings. • Reread the formative evaluations of the strengths and weaknesses of the group and the leader. • Think about your personal evolution in the framework of your group this term. **STEP 1: Assessment** List points, principles, or events — positive and negative — that had the greatest impact on you in this group work. __________ __________ __________ __________ **STEP 2: Recommendations** Draw up the list of recommendations that you would make to yourself so that your next participation in group work (in a course or in your professional life) is a more productive and enriching experience. __________ __________ __________ __________

8.5.4 Comments on Grading Students

We will now briefly consider the problem of grading students who submit work done in a group.

If a group functions well and all of its members become equally committed, they generally do not object to receiving a group grade for their assignment.

However, you must assign individual grades if some members of a group unduly take advantage of the work of the others. You must also do so for assignments or activities that involve only one member. For example, you can individually grade the work of the leader by making a compromise between his or her own judgment and the results of the two formative evaluations of the leader (weeks 5 and 9).

The weekly minutes kept by each group member can also be graded individually. Here again, the grade can be a compromise between the grade given by the group members and the grade that you give for the two or three reports turned in by each member during the term.

In addition, you can also individually penalize group members for each meeting that they miss without a valid excuse.

Combining these individual grades with the group grades given for the final report, the presentation at the end of the session, and so forth will result in different final grades for each member. Each student will thus get an overall grade that will take into account his or her commitment in the group and the quality of the work he or she did.

Review

Distribution of energy in a good work group

In a good group:

- All members share and value the same goal (productive energy, E_p).
- There is a constant climate of harmonious interpersonal exchanges (solidarity energy, E_s).
- Members know how to surmount obstacles that inhibit the good functioning of the group (maintenance energy, E_m).
- Each member truly commits (ideally no residual energy, E_r).

Recommendations for the initial sessions of group work

- Establish a good relationship between the group members.
- Compare the individual perceptions of the shared goal.
- Define and share the tasks.
- Make sure that all of the group members become involved.

Recommendations for effective participation of group members

- Ensure that every member participates as both "transmitter" and "receiver."
- Address the group and not one single individual.
- Participate in a positive way.
- Participate in the leadership.
- Pay attention to the others.
- Communicate your feelings and impressions.

Characteristics of an effective meeting

Preparing for a meeting

- The leader prepares the agenda, plans the approximate time frame for each item, and makes sure the secretary and each of the members have done the work assigned to them.
- The secretary writes up the minutes of the preceding meeting and gives them to the leader at least one day before the meeting date.
- Each group member does the work assigned to him or her.

Conducting a meeting

- The participants must be welcomed.
- The meeting must begin on time.
- The leader has the other members approve the agenda and the minutes of the preceding meeting, makes sure that each can speak freely, and runs the meeting according to the planned time frame.
- The secretary takes notes, in order to write up a report for the meeting.
- Each member participates in a positive way.

Closing a meeting

- The leader summarizes the work accomplished.
- The leader regularly proposes that the group evaluate how it is functioning.

Proposal for a training strategy for group work

- Form groups of four or five members by drawing lots, or let natural groups form, according to the situation.
- Exercise 1: "Meeting the Members of My Group."
- Readings or lectures: The distribution of energy in a good work group. Holding effective meetings.
- Exercise 2: Choosing a leader and establishing a calendar that includes the weekly rotation of the meeting secretaries.
- Exercises 3 and 4: Formative evaluations of the strengths and weaknesses of the group and the leader.
- Exercise 5: Individual assessment at the end of the term.

CHAPTER 9

EVALUATING YOUR TEACHING

A new course is somewhat like a prototype that is tested in a laboratory. In class, all of the components of a course are tested — the quantity and validity of the material, the distribution of work in the term, the choice of textbook, teaching methods, and materials, and the choice of means to evaluate the students. The course also tests the professor's general teaching abilities.

In this chapter, we propose two ways to conduct a *formative evaluation* of your course — an evaluation to elicit feedback from the students on each of the components that we have analyzed in terms of improving of a course.

The first formative evaluation form that we propose is an *informal evaluation, around midterm,* based on your students' answers to two open-ended questions. The objective of this evaluation is to gather information in order to make minor adjustments to improve certain aspects for the second half of the term.

The second form of the formative evaluation is a *more formal evaluation, at the end of the course,* using your students' answers to closed questions. The results of this evaluation help you improve your course and teaching for subsequent terms.

9.1 Informal Midterm Formative Evaluation

The first form of course evaluation, which usually takes place between the fourth and the sixth weeks, allows you to gather, orally or in writing, information that can help you make immediate adjustments or corrections to improve the remainder of the course. You ask the students just two questions, similar to the questions below.

- What are two or three points that you have liked most in the course?
- What are two or three points that have caused difficulties and that should be improved? Can you make any suggestions for improving them?

You compile the results of this survey and, the following week, discuss the comments in class. This discussion should lead to adjustments that may allow immediate improvement of certain aspects of the course.

Such a formative evaluation exerts, according to the individual cases, different beneficial influences, such as:

- a perceptible improvement in the climate of your class,
- a strengthening of the ties between you and your students,
- an increase in the participation and motivation of the students,

- an improvement in the organization of the course (revised timetable, clearer instructions, etc.), and
- an improvement in your teaching abilities.

9.1.1 Method

Table 9.1 shows a four-step approach to conducting a midterm informal formative evaluation.

Table 9.1 Method for the midterm formative evaluation

Steps	Activities
Step 1	**Inform the students of the objectives of this evaluation** (2 minutes) At the beginning of the fourth class, for example, you announce to your students your intention to gather comments on *what they like so far* in the course and *what they would like to see improved.* You tell them that, as much as possible, you will consider their comments and try to make the necessary adjustments to improve subsequent sessions. You also tell them that you will comment on what you like about the students and on what you would like to see improve. You express your hope that this sharing of comments will result in a beneficial discussion.
Step 2	**Gather student comments, in writing** (5 minutes) Ask the students to write down, *individually, one or two points that they particularly like about the course.* These points can relate to any aspect of the course or to you. Also ask them to write down *one or two points that they would like to see improved* in the course.
Step 3	**Compile the results of the survey** (30-60 minutes) Between the fourth and the fifth classes, you *succinctly compile, in two columns,* the good points and the points to improve as identified by the students. You regroup these comments by *subject* — textbook, lab work, teaching abilities, etc. You determine the frequency of comments on any one subject, taking into account only the comments provided by a significant number of students and ignoring isolated comments. You transfer these comments onto a *transparency,* beginning with the most frequent. Then, it's your turn to *evaluate student learning behaviors:* attention in class, preparation in the laboratories, degree of participation, completion of exercises, absenteeism, or whatever is appropriate. You write down these observations in two columns as well, from the most to the least important, and transfer them onto a transparency.

Table 9.1 Continued

Step 4	**Discuss the results in class with the students** (15 minutes) At the beginning of the fifth class, you show your students the transparency of the positive points and the points to improve that they have identified. You show them what you can improve now and what you cannot change, *giving your reasons.* After that, you open the matter up for *discussion.* Then, you do the same thing with your observations about your students.

9.1.2 Example

To give you a more concrete idea of the type of results a midterm formative evaluation can provide, we reproduce, in Example 9.1, the comments obtained by one professor.

The professor who received the comments presented in Example 9.1 can be pleased with the general organization of his class: the textbook, the laboratory sessions, and the means of evaluation seem to work well. In addition, the students like his general communication skills.

On the other hand, he must admit that he could take more care in the structure of his lectures. So he resolves to post the outline of each lecture on the board at the beginning of class and to provide the students with a review of the points he judgese most important.

Example 9.1 Comments obtained by one professor from an informal midterm formative evaluation

	Comments	Frequency
Positive points	• Textbook: well done; exhaustive; detailed.	19
	• Class: interesting; good atmosphere; a certain humor; professor knows how to capture attention.	19
	• Laboratory sessions: adequate; close tie with the course; well-prepared; competent and cooperative laboratory personnel.	15
	• Professor: competent.	10
	• Means of evaluation: good.	9
	• Professor: interested in this course and wants to make the students understand the material; makes students participate; asks questions.	9

Example 9.1 Continued

Points to improve	• Professor: sometimes dwells too much on small details and does not emphasize difficult points enough; does not give enough prominence to the important points; beginnings of classes slow and ends of classes often accelerated and abrupt.	14
	• Lacks structure; should give the class plan at the beginning of each session; should situate each of the subjects better within the corpus.	13
	• Insufficient office hours for the project.	11
	• Work at the board lacks order and legibility; too many transparencies, too overloaded, often impossible to copy.	10
	• Textbook lacks exercises and examples.	8
	• Some laboratory sessions too long.	6

The professor also resolves to work at the board in a more ordered and legible manner. And he decides to give the transparencies at the end of each class to a class representative, who will be in charge of making photocopies for students who want them.

So that his students can consult with him more easily about their projects, the professor agrees to move his half-day of office time.

In his comments, the professor underscores the quality of the students' participation and commitment, which engenders a climate favorable to communication. He also mentions their punctuality and their regular attendance, despite the difficult time schedule (Mondays from 8:30 to 11:30 a.m.).

However, he shares his impression that they are not reading the recommended chapters after each class, which exerts a direct negative influence on the preparation for the laboratory sessions. He points out that the laboratory sessions are not so long, but rather that the students are rather poorly prepared for them. He takes advantage of the moment to remind the students that, in accordance with the work distribution for the course (3-3-3), they should be doing an average of 3 hours of personal weekly work, in addition to attending class (3 hours) and participating in the laboratory sessions (3 hours).

As you can see, formative evaluation of teaching brings out positive and encouraging aspects, but it also underscores the necessity for both students and professor to make certain adjustments to improve the rest of the course — adjustments that are immediately useful to everybody.

9.1.3 Variations of the Procedure

We propose below three variations of the informal formative evaluation just described:

- *direct discussion* with students;
- formation of a *committee of class representatives;*
- use of a *colleague* or *teaching expert.*

Direct Discussion With Students. This first variation is closely related to the basic method, except for the matter of compiling students' comments.

You ask the students to form teams of four or five and for each team to answer the two questions from the basic method (two positive points and two points to improve). After that, you reassemble all of the students and the reporter from each team summarizes the comments of his or her team. You copy these statements onto the board, without commenting on them. If the same statement occurs several times, you write down the number of occurrences. This compilation is usually very short, because there are often correlations among the comments from the different teams.

You then classify the comments in decreasing order of frequency and discuss with your students ways to improve.

The fact that the whole procedure takes place in a single class period, without any intermediary or delay, constitutes the main advantage of this variation.

However, this procedure is not recommended for beginning professors. It's important to have some teaching experience and a certain assurance to face the students' comments directly, without having time to think about them.

Formation of a Committee of Class Representatives. In this second variation, you invite the students to form a committee of three or four class representatives, whose task is to gather input from their classmates. You can then regularly convene this committee — once a month, for example — to discuss the evolution of the course and any difficulties. This variation, of course, requires a greater time investment, since there are three meetings per term, without counting the whole class sessions that are sometimes necessary.

Use of a Colleague or Teaching Expert. This third variation uses a source other than the students for feedback on the course and your teaching. You ask a more experienced colleague, who knows the course well and who is reputed to be a good teacher, or a teaching expert — a consultant in higher education, for example — to observe one or several class sessions. Although this visitor may have difficulty commenting on the pedagogical organization of the class from observation alone, he or she can easily comment on the your teaching and how you:

- set up before class,
- introduce your subject,
- structure your lecture,
- vary your voice, gestures, and eye contact,
- ask questions,
- answer questions,
- summarize the important ideas, and
- give directions for exercises and assignments.

Although in this variation you do not solicit input from your students, they can benefit from the improvements that results from your visitor's observations.

9.2 A More Formal Final Formative Evaluation

We now propose another formative evaluation, one that takes place at the end of the term (usually between the tenth and the last weeks of class). It is based on a questionnaire consisting of closed statements only. This activity gives the students an opportunity to provide an overall assessment of the class and you.

This evaluation will not be directly useful to them, of course, since the term will be over, but their comments will help you improve the course the next time you teach it. The students thus contribute to improving courses to come, just as students before them contributed to improving the course(s) they've just taken.

This type of evaluation can be used at midterm as well, with very large groups, because it's easier and quicker to compile the results than with open-ended evaluations. Here again, these results can start a discussion with your students about how you can modify your class and your teaching.

9.2.1 Aspects Evaluated

Aspects most often evaluated with student questionnaires are:

- competence of the professor,
- structure of the course,
- the professor's communication skills,
- professor-student relations,
- means of evaluating the students,
- teaching materials,
- laboratory or discussion sessions, and
- general characteristics of the professor and the class.

In Table 9.2, we present some standard statements for each of these aspects.

Table 9.2 Standard statements used for term-end course evaluations

Competence of the professor	• The professor has a thorough knowledge of the course material. • The professor knows well the material well that he teaches. • The professor controls the material that he teaches.
Structure of the course	• This professor prepares his classes well. • Each class session is well-prepared. • Generally, the class is well-organized. • The material was distributed well throughout the term. • The work was distributed well throughout the term. • The work required by this course is justified by the number of credits.
Communication skills	• The professor knows how to capture and hold the students' attention. • The professor explains clearly. • The professor knows how to emphasize the important points of the course. • The professor answers students' questions clearly. • The professor regularly provides appropriate examples to help students understand the material.
Relationships with the students	• In his conduct, the professor has shown respect for the students. • The professor demonstrates an interest in teaching this course.

Table 9.2 Continued

Relationships with the students	• The professor appears concerned about constantly improving this course. • The professor is open to student comments and criticisms about this course.
Means of evaluating learning	• The evaluation criteria were communicated from the very beginning of the term. • The weighting assigned to each one of the aspects evaluated (assignments, work, tests) is appropriate. • The test questions focused on the important points of the course. • After a test, the professor takes the time to go over the difficulties experienced by the students.
Teaching materials	• The recommended documentation (textbooks, handouts, etc.) covers the different aspects of the course well. • The purchase of the recommended works is fully justified by the use of them in the course. • The recommended works are pedagogically well-designed: they facilitate comprehension of the material. • When the professor uses the board, he does it in a legible and orderly way. • The professor designs transparencies well and uses them appropriately.
Laboratory sessions	• There are obvious links between the material in class and the laboratory sessions. • The instructions for each session are precise and complete. • The time allotted is sufficient so that the students attain the objectives of each session. • The accompanying documents are complete and adequate. • The requirements relative to the completion of the reports are reasonable and match the course objectives.
Overall evaluation	• Generally, I liked this class. • This class allowed me to achieve significant learning. • This class made me want to learn more about the material. • Generally, I liked this professor. This professor's teaching is stimulating.

9.2.2 Preparing a Questionnaire

If you want to construct a questionnaire with closed statements to obtain student input, you should:

- choose the statements,
- limit the number of statements to about 20,
- choose an appropriate evaluation scale, and
- write the directions to place at the top of the questionnaire.

It's important to use short, unambiguous statements, each one focusing on a single aspect of instruction. All of the statements must be affirmative sentences, so that the evaluation scale applies in the same way to all the statements.

In addition, it's pointless to write a questionnaire composed of 50 statements, for example, because your students will tire of filling it out and will lose their concentration as well as their motivation to answer objectively. If you choose about 20 statements, that should be enough for the students to evaluate the important aspects of the class. If you want, you can include several lines at the end of the questionnaire, so that students can write down their suggestions; if you neglect any important aspects of the course, students are likely to touch upon those in their suggestions.

You should use an evaluation scale of *four* points, asking the students to indicate for each of the statements whether they are:

1. completely in disagreement;
2. somewhat in disagreement;
3. somewhat in agreement;
4. completely in agreement.

It's best to avoid a fifth option, such as "neither agree nor disagree," since a neutral position is easy to choose and difficult to interpret.

However, an evaluation scale should allow for the possibility that a student cannot evaluate a given statement by allowing him or her to indicate that the statement "does not apply."

Finally, the directions at the top of the questionnaire must clearly indicate what you expect of your students, as the "directions" in Example 9.2 show.

9.3 Administrative Evaluation

Many colleges and universities invite their professors to distribute teaching evaluation forms to their students at the end of the term. Most often, these evaluations serve administrative purposes: the results, kept in the professor's file, can be used for summative purposes, as in promotion and tenure decisions.

Administrative teaching evaluations are sometimes used to obtain information to supplement the judgments of colleagues who were asked to evaluate a professor's teaching, course organization, materials, and so forth.

The teaching evaluations in this chapter can in no way serve administrative purposes. These evaluation forms are intended simply to help improve a course.

If you are interested in the evaluation of teaching for administrative purposes, you'll find references on this subject in the bibliography and an example of a basic questionnaire in Example 9.2 (on the next page).

Example 9.2 Basic structure of a term-end teaching evaluation questionnaire

(Name of the institution)

TEACHING EVALUATION QUESTIONNAIRE

Term and year Fall ______ Winter ______ Summer ______ 19 ___

Number of the course ______________________________

Title of the course ______________________________

Name of the professor ______________________________

No. of the group (or section) ______________________________

DIRECTIONS

- Answer this questionnaire individually and anonymously.
- The results of this questionnaire will be used to improve the course.
- Indicate how each statement below describes the professor or the course, using the following scale:

1, if you are **completely in disagreement** with the statement;
2, if you are **somewhat in disagreement** with the statement;
3, if you are **somewhat in agreement** with the statement;
4, if you are **completely in agreement** with the statement.

Put "X" if the statement does not apply.

(List of the questions)

1. ______________________ 4. ______________________

2. ______________________ 5. ______________________

3. ______________________ 6. ______________________

And so forth for all of the questions.

SUGGESTIONS TO IMPROVE THE COURSE

____

____

____

Review

Informal midterm formative evaluation with open questions

- This evaluation takes place between the fourth and sixth weeks.
- You ask students to identify two positive points and two points to improve (with suggestions for improvement) concerning the class or you.
- You compile the results.
- The following week, you discuss the comments with your students.
- You also comment on the behaviors and attitudes of your students.
- The comments lead to a discussion that may result in improvements that benefit you and your students through the rest of the course.

Variations

- Gather the students' comments, compile them on the spot, and discuss them immediately with the students.
- Form a committee of students who meet with the professor, once a month, to discuss the course.
- Invite a colleague or teaching expert to observe your class.

Formal term-end formative evaluation with closed statements

If you want to create a teaching evaluation questionnaire, you must:

- define which aspects of teaching the students should evaluate;
- choose statements for each one of these aspects (about 20 in all);
- use a four-point evaluation scale;
- write directions for the questionnaire.

CONCLUSION

Contrary to common belief, teaching is a complex task that requires sometimes diverse qualities of the professor. A professor must have the talents and competencies of both a *knowledge engineer* — when preparing activities for a course — and an *artist* — when working with the students in class.

On the one hand, teaching requires meticulous preparation:

- You analyze your teaching situation.
- You determine the relative importance and difficulty of the subjects to cover.
- You write the objectives you want your students to attain.
- You choose and construct the means of evaluating their progress.
- You choose the appropriate teaching methods and prepare the necessary activities and material.
- You write the course syllabus, the course outline, and the lesson plans.

On the other hand, teaching requires the acquisition, use, and improvement of certain skills essential to effective instruction. Thus, the first class — the first contact between you and your students — is of vital importance. You need a certain charisma, a lot of imagination, a contagious enthusiasm for your subject, and a high-level sense of organization in order to win over the students right from the start. You need to gain their confidence and arouse their interest.

Teaching based on *lectures* is not simple: you must be effective, structured, clear, and intellectually captivating. You must know how to introduce, conclude, emphasize the essential ideas, provide examples, verify understanding, answer questions, and so on.

Using *group work* is equally complex, because you must create a learning environment that allows for evaluation and maximizes the use of productive energy, solidarity energy, and maintenance energy within the groups, while minimizing residual energy. To do this, you must be a supervisor, project manager, motivator, and referee.

In addition, you must always remember that you will never be able to learn for your students, and that you prepare and organize a course not for yourself, but for the students. Consequently, you should place the students as much as possible in the center of the intellectual processes — the objectives — of your course.

It may seem odd, but we believe that the most important goal in teaching is not to transmit knowledge, but to make the students want to learn in a particular field and become personally involved in their learning. You are no longer the simple dispenser of knowledge of times past, trying to transmit as much as possible about as many subjects as possible in a limited period of time. You are somebody who should try to spread the "virus" of your subject area.

The period of encyclopedic academic training is past. In the society of the third millennium, students will have to learn to be intellectually active, independently and continuously, throughout their lives. You can help them do just that.

BIBLIOGRAPHY

Adderley, Kenneth, *et al. Project Methods in Higher Education.* Society for Research into Higher Education, Working Party on Teaching Methods, Techniques Group. London: Society for Research into Higher Education, 1975.

Ausubel, David Paul. *The Psychology of Meaningful Verbal Learning: An Introduction to School Learning.* New York: Grune & Stratton, 1963.

Axelrod, Joseph. *The University Teacher as Artist.* San Francisco: Jossey-Bass, 1973.

Barrows, Howard S., and Robyn M. Tamblyn. *Problem-Based Learning: An Approach to Medical Education.* New York: Springer Publishing, 1980.

Barrows, Howard S. "A Taxonomy of Problem-Based Learning Methods." *Medical Education,* 20:6 (November 1986), pp. 481-486.

Barrows, Howard S. "Problem-Based Self-Directed Learning." *Journal of the American Medical Association,* 250:22 (December 1983), pp. 481-486.

Berliner, David C. "In Pursuit of the Expert Pedagogue." *Educational Researcher,* August-September 1986, pp. 5-13.

Bligh, Donald A. *What's the Use of Lectures?* Exeter (UK): D.A. and B. Bligh, 1971.

Bloom, Benjamin Samuel, Max D. Engelhart, Edward J. Furst, W.H. Hill, and David R. Krathwohl, eds. *Taxonomy of Educational Objectives: The Classification of Educational Goals. Handbook I, Cognitive Domain.* 1st ed. New York: David McKay, 1956.

Bloom, Benjamin Samuel, J. Thomas Hastings, and George F. Madaus. *Handbook on Formative and Summative Evaluation of Student Learning.* New York: McGraw-Hill, 1974.

Bock, Dorothy Joleen, and Ernest W. Tompkins. *Learning Laboratories: Individualized Adult Learning.* New York: Library Journal, 1980.

Boud, David, ed. *Developing Student Autonomy in Learning*. 2nd ed. London, New York: Kogan Page, Nichols, 1988.

Boud, David, Jeffrey Dunn, and Elizabeth Hegarty-Hazel. *Teaching in Laboratories*. Exeter: Society for Research into Higher Education and NFER-NELSON, 1986.

Bouton, Clark, and Russell Y. Garth, eds. *Learning in Groups*. San Francisco: Jossey-Bass, 1983.

Braskamp, Larry A., Dale C. Brandenburg, and John C. Ory. *Evaluating Teaching Effectiveness: A Practical Guide*. Beverly Hills, CA: Sage Publications, 1984.

Brown, George. *Lecturing and Explaining*. London: Methuen, 1978.

Brown, George. *Microteaching: A Programme of Teaching Skills*. London: Methuen; New York: distributed by Harper & Row, 1975.

Brown, George, and Madeleine Atkins. *Effective Teaching in Higher Education*. London, New York: Methuen, 1987.

Brown, James W., Richard B. Lewis, and Fred F. Harcleroad. *AV Instruction: Technology, Media, and Methods*. 6th ed. New York: McGraw-Hill, 1983.

Browne, M. Neil, and Stuart M. Keeley. *Asking the Right Questions: A Guide to Critical Thinking*. 3d ed. Englewood Cliffs, NJ: Prentice-Hall, 1990.

Bullard, John R., and Calvin E. Mether. *Audiovisual Fundamentals: Basic Equipment Operation and Simple Materials Production*. 3rd ed. Dubuque, IA: W.C. Brown, 1984.

Calderhead, James, and Peter Gates. *Conceptualizing Reflection in Teacher Development*. London, Washington, DC: Falmer Press, 1993.

Carkhuff, Robert R. *The Art of Problem-Solving: A Guide for Developing Problem-Solving Skills for Parents, Teachers, Counselors, and Administrators*. Amherst, MA: Human Resource Development Press, 1974.

Cashin, William. *Improving Lectures*. IDEA Paper no. 14. Manhattan, KS: Center for Faculty Evaluation and Development, Kansas State University, 1985.

Change Magazine. *Guide to Effective Teaching: A National Report on 81 Outstanding College Teachers and How They Teach: Lectures, Computers, Case Studies, Peer Teaching, Simulations, Self-Pacing, Multimedia, Field Study, Problem Solving, and Research*. New Rochelle, NY: Change Magazine Press, 1978.

Chickering, Arthur W. *Experience and Learning: An Introduction to Experiential Learning*. New Rochelle, NY: Change Magazine Press, 1977.

Chickering, Arthur W., and Zelda F. Gamson, eds. *Applying the Seven Principles for Good Practice in Undergraduate Education.* San Francisco: Jossey-Bass, 1991.

Christensen, C. Roland, and Abby J. Hansen. *Teaching and the Case Method: Texts, Cases, and Readings.* Boston: Harvard Business School, 1987.

Clark, Richard, and G. Salomon. "Media in Teaching." In Merlin C. Wittrock, ed., *Handbook of Research on Teaching.* 3rd ed. New York: Macmillan; London: Collier Macmillan, 1986, pp. 464-475.

Clarke, Edward G. "Grading Seminar Performance." *College Teaching,* 33:3 (Summer 1985), pp. 129-133.

Clarke, John H. "Building a Lecture That Really Works." *The Education Digest,* 53:2 (October 1987), pp. 52-55.

Cross, K. Patricia, and Thomas A. Angelo. *Classroom Assessment Techniques: A Handbook for College Teachers.* 2nd ed. San Francisco: Jossey-Bass, 1993.

Davis, Barbara Gross. *Tools for Teaching.* San Francisco: Jossey-Bass, 1993.

Duffy, Thomas M., and Robert Waller, eds. *Designing Usable Texts.* Orlando: Academic Press, 1985.

Dunkin, Michael J. *The International Encyclopedia of Teaching and Teacher Education.* Oxford (UK), New York: Pergamon Press, 1987.

Dwyer, Francis M. *Strategies for Improving Visual Learning: A Handbook for the Effective Selection, Design, and Use of Visualized Materials.* State College, PA: Pennsylvania State University, Learning Services, 1978.

Eble, Kenneth E. *The Craft of Teaching: A Guide to Mastering the Professor's Art.* 2nd ed. San Francisco: Jossey-Bass, 1988.

Ericksen, Stanford C. *The Essence of Good Teaching: Helping Students Learn and Remember What They Learn.* San Francisco: Jossey-Bass, 1984.

Frederick, Peter J. "The Dreaded Discussion: Ten Ways to Start." *College Teaching,* 29:3 (Summer 1981), pp. 109-114. Reprinted in Rose Ann Neff and Maryellen Weimer, eds., *Classroom Communication: Collected Readings for Effective Discussion and Questioning,* Madison, WI: Magna Publications, 1989, pp. 9-17.

Frederick, Peter J. "The Lively Lecture — 8 Variations." *College Teaching,* 34:2 (Spring 1986), pp. 43-50.

Fuhrmann, Barbara Schneider, and Anthony F. Grasha. *A Practical Handbook for College Teachers.* Boston: Little, Brown, 1983.

Gage, N.L. (Nathaniel Lees). *The Scientific Basis of the Art of Teaching.* New York: Teachers College Press, Columbia University, 1978.

Gagne, Robert Mills. *The Conditions of Learning and Theory of Instruction.* 5th ed. New York: Holt, Rinehart and Winston, 1985.

Gibbs, Graham. *Teaching More Students: Problems and Course Design Strategies.* Tome 1. Oxford: Polytechnics and Colleges Funding Council, 1992.

Gibbs, Graham. *Teaching More Students: Lecturing to More Students.* Tome 2. Oxford: Polytechnics and Colleges Funding Council, 1992.

Gibbs, Graham. *Teaching More Students: Discussion With More Students.* Tome 3. Oxford: Polytechnics and Colleges Funding Council, 1992.

Gibbs, Graham. *Teaching More Students: Assessing More Students.* Tome 4. Oxford: Polytechnics and Colleges Funding Council, 1992.

Gibbs, Graham. *Teaching More Students: Independent Learning With More Students.* Tome 5. Oxford: Polytechnics and Colleges Funding Council, 1992.

Gronlund, Norman Edward. *How to Write and Use Instructional Objectives.* 4th ed. New York: Macmillan; Toronto: Collier Macmillan Canada, 1991.

Gullette, Margaret Morganroth, ed. *The Art and Craft of Teaching.* Cambridge, MA: Harvard-Danforth Center for Teaching and Learning, 1982.

Harrow, Anita J. *A Taxonomy of the Psychomotor Domain: A Guide for Developing Behavioral Objectives.* New York: David McKay, 1972.

Hart, Lois B. *Saying Goodbye: Ending a Group Experience.* 2nd ed. King of Prussia, PA: Organization Design and Development, 1989.

Hart, Lois B. *Saying Hello: Getting Your Group Started.* 2nd ed. King of Prussia, PA: Organization Design and Development, 1989.

Hartley, James. *Designing Instructional Text.* 2nd ed. London: Kogan Page; New York: Nichols, 1985.

Herr, Kay. *Improving Teaching and Learning in Large Classes: A Practical Manual.* Fort Collins, CO: Colorado State University, Office of Instructional Services, 1985.

Hiemstra, Roger, and Burton Sisco. *Individualizing Instruction: Making Learning Personal, Empowering, and Successful.* San Francisco: Jossey-Bass, 1990.

Hitchcock, D. *Critical Thinking: A Guide to Evaluating Information.* Toronto: Methuen, 1983.

Hutchings, Pat, and Allen Wutzdorff, eds. *Knowing and Doing: Learning Through Experience.* San Francisco: Jossey-Bass, 1988.

Hyman, Ronald T. *Improving Discussion Leadership.* New York: Teachers College Press, 1980.

Hyman, Ronald T. *Questioning in the College Classroom.* IDEA Paper no. 7. Manhattan, KS: Center for Faculty Evaluation and Development, Kansas State University, 1982.

Hyman, Ronald T. *Strategic Questioning.* Englewood Cliffs, NJ: Prentice-Hall, 1979.

Jacobs, Lucy Cheser, and Clinton I. Chase. *Developing and Using Tests Effectively: A Guide for Faculty.* San Francisco: Jossey-Bass, 1992.

Jaques, David. *Learning in Groups.* London; Dover (UK): Croom Helm, 1984.

Jenson, Eric. *Student Success Secrets.* 3rd ed. New York: Barron's Educational Series, 1989.

Johnson, Glenn Ross. *First Steps to Excellence in College Teaching.* Madison, WI: Magna Publications, 1990.

Jonassen, David H., ed. *The Technology of Text: Principles for Structuring, Designing and Displaying Text.* 2 vols. Englewood Cliffs, NJ: Education Technology Publications, 1982 and 1985.

Jones, John E., and William L. Bearley. *Energizers for Training and Conferences.* King of Prussia, PA: Organization Design and Development, 1989.

Joyce, Bruce R., and Marsha Weil. *Models of Teaching.* 4th ed. Boston: Allyn and Bacon, 1992.

Klausmeier, Herbert J. *Learning and Teaching Concepts: A Strategy for Testing Applications of Theory.* New York: Academic Press, 1980.

Klein, Hans E., ed. *Case Method Research and Application: New Vistas.* Selected papers of the Sixth International Conference on Case Method Research and Case Method Application. Needham, MA: World Association for Case Method Research and Application, 1989.

Knowles, Malcolm Shepherd. *Using Learning Contracts.* San Francisco: Jossey-Bass, 1986.

Kolb, David A. *Experiential Learning: Experience as the Source of Learning and Development.* Englewood Cliffs, NJ: Prentice-Hall, 1984.

Krathwohl, David R., Benjamin Samuel Bloom, and Bertram B. Masia, eds. *Taxonomy of Educational Objectives: The Classification of Educational Goals. Handbook II, Affective Domain.* 1st ed. New York: David McKay, 1964.

Lefrancois, Guy R. *Psychology for Teaching: A Bear Always Faces the Front.* 6th ed. Belmont, CA: Wadsworth Publishing, 1988.

Lowman, Joseph. *Mastering the Techniques of Teaching.* San Francisco: Jossey-Bass, 1984.

Lowther, Malcolm A., Joan S. Stark, and Gretchen G. Martens. *Preparing Course Syllabi for Improved Communication.* Ann Arbor, MI: National Center for Research to Improve Postsecondary Teaching and Learning, University of Michigan, 1989.

Mager, Robert F. *Preparing Instructional Objectives.* Rev. 2nd ed. Belmont, CA: Pitman Management & Training, 1984.

Marsh, Herbert W. "Student Evaluations of University Teaching — Dimensionality, Reliability, Validity, Potential Biases and Utility. *Journal of Educational Psychology,* 76:5 (1984), pp. 707-754.

Martin, Barbara L., and Leslie J. Briggs. *The Affective and Cognitive Domains: Integration for Instruction and Research.* Englewood Cliffs, NJ: Educational Technology Publications, 1986.

McKeachie, Wilbert J. *Teaching and Learning in the College Classroom: A Review of the Research Literature.* Ann Arbor, MI: National Center for Research to Improve Postsecondary Teaching and Learning, University of Michigan, 1986.

McKeachie, Wilbert J. *Teaching Tips: A Guidebook for the Beginning College Teacher.* 8th ed. Lexington, MA: D.C. Heath, 1986.

McMillan, James H., ed. *Assessing Students' Learning.* San Francisco: Jossey-Bass, 1988.

Millman, Jason. *Handbook of Teacher Evaluation.* Beverly Hills, CA: Sage Publications, 1981.

Meyers, Chet, and Thomas B. Jones. *Promoting Active Learning: Strategies for the College Classroom.* San Francisco: Jossey-Bass, 1993.

Neff, Rose Ann, and Maryellen Weimer, eds. *Classroom Communication: Collected Readings for Effective Discussion and Questioning.* Madison, WI: Magna Publications, 1989.

Neff, Rose Ann, and Maryellen Weimer, eds. *Teaching College: Collected Readings for the New Instructor.* Madison, WI: Magna Publications, 1989.

Neufeld, Victor R., and Howard S. Barrows. "McMaster Philosophy: An Approach to Medical Education." *Journal of Medical Education,* 49 (November 1974), pp. 1,040-1,050.

Nickerson, Raymond S., David Perkins, and Edward E. Smith. *The Teaching of Thinking*. Hillsdale, NJ: Lawrence Erlbaum Associates, 1985.

Paul, Richard. *Critical Thinking: What Every Person Needs to Survive in a Rapidly Changing World*. 2nd ed. Santa Rosa, CA: Foundation for Critical Thinking, 1992.

Perrott, Elizabeth. *Microteaching in Higher Education: Research, Development, and Practice*. Guildford (UK): Society for Research into Higher Education at the University of Surrey, 1977.

Pigors, Paul, and Faith Pigors. *The Pigors Incident Process of Case Study*. Englewood Cliff,s NJ: Educational Technology Publications, 1980.

Posner, George J., and Alan N. Rudnitsky. *Course Design: A Guide to Curriculum Development for Teachers*. 3rd ed. New York: Longman, 1986.

Postlethwait, Samuel N., Joseph D. Novak, and Hallard T. Murray, Jr. *The Audio-Tutorial Approach to Learning: Through Independent Study and Integrated Experiences*. 3rd ed. Minneapolis: Burgess, 1972.

Ronstadd, R. *The Art of Case Analysis: A Guide to the Diagnosis of Business Situations*. 2nd ed. Dover (UK): Lord Publishing, 1980.

Rosenshine, Barak, and Robert Stevens. "Teaching Functions." In Merlin C. Wittrock, ed., *Handbook of Research on Teaching*. 3rd ed. New York: Macmillan; London: Collier Macmillan, 1986. pp. 376-389.

Rudduck, Jean. *Learning Through Small Group Discussion: A Study of Seminar Work in Higher Education*. Guildford (UK): Society for Research into Higher Education at the University of Surrey, 1978.

Ryan, Bruce A. *PSI — Keller's Personalized System of Instruction: An Appraisal*. Washington DC: American Psychological Association, 1974.

Schmidt, Henk G. "Problem-Based Learning: Rationale and Description." *Medical Education*, 17:1 (January 1983), pp. 11-16.

Schmidt, Henk G., *et al.*, eds. *New Directions for Medical Education: Problem-Based Learning and Community-Oriented Medical Education*. New York: Springer-Verlag, 1989.

Sherman, J. Gilmour, and Robert S. Ruskin. *The Personalized System of Instruction*. Englewood Cliffs, NJ: Educational Technology Publications, 1978.

Stark, Joan S., Malcolm A. Lowther, Michael P. Ryan, Sally Smith Bomotti, Michele Genthon, and C. Lynne Haven. *Reflections on Course Planning: Faculty and Students Consider Influences and Goals*. Ann Arbor, MI: Na-

National Center for Research to Improve Postsecondary Teaching and Learning, University of Michigan, 1988.

Steinaker, Norman, and M. Robert Bell. *The Experiential Taxonomy: A New Approach to Teaching and Learning.* New York: Academic Press, 1979.

Stodt-Lopez, Barbara. *Word Choice and Narration: Artistic Language Use in Academic Lectures.* Norwood, NJ: Ablex Publications, 1993.

Stromberg, Steven F., ed. *Strategies for Active Teaching and Learning in University Classrooms.* Minneapolis: University of Minnesota, 1986.

Stufflebeam, Daniel L., *et al. Educational Evaluation and Decision-Making.* Bloomington, IN: Phi Delta Kappa National Study Committee on Evaluation, 1977, 1971.

Stufflebeam, Daniel L., and Anthony J. Shinkfield. *Systematic Evaluation: A Self-Instructional Guide to Theory and Practice.* Boston: Kluer-Nijhoff, 1985.

Taylor, Charles Alfred. *The Art and Science of Lecture Demonstration.* Bristol (UK), Philadelphia: Adam Hilger, 1988.

Thiagarajan, Sivasailam, and Harold D. Stolovitch. *Instructional Simulation Games.* Englewood Cliffs, NJ: Educational Technology Publications, 1978.

Weaver, Richard L., II. "Effective Lecturing Techniques: Alternatives to Classroom Boredom." *New Directions in Teaching,* 7 (Winter 1982), Bowling Green State University, pp. 31-39. Reprinted in Rose Ann Neff and Maryellen Weimer, eds. *Teaching College: Collected Readings for the New Instructor,* Madison, WI: Magna Publications, pp. 65-68.

Weimer, Maryellen. "Course Materials Review: A Checklist." *The Teaching Professor,* 1:6 (August 1987), pp. 3-4.

Weimer, Maryellen. "The First Day of Class: Advice and Ideas." *The Teaching Professor,* 3:7 (August/September 1989), pp. 1-2.

Weimer, Maryellen. "Meet Your Professor." *The Teaching Professor,* 3:1 (January 1989), p. 2.

Weimer, Maryellen. "One Syllabus That Encourages Thinking, Not Just Learning." *The Teaching Professor,* 1:6 (August 1987), p. 5.

Weimer, Maryellen Gleason, ed. *Teaching Large Classes Well.* San Francisco: Jossey-Bass, 1987.

Weimer, Maryellen. "What to Do When Students Don't Do the Reading." *The Teaching Professor,* 3:4 (April 1989), pp. 1-2.

Weimer, Maryellen, Joan L. Parrett, and Mary-Margaret Kerns. *How Am I Teaching? Forms and Activities for Acquiring Instructional Input.* Madison, WI: Magna Publications, 1988.

Wittrock, Merlin C., ed. *Handbook of Research on Teaching.* 3rd ed. New York: Macmillan; London: Collier Macmillan, 1986.

Zenger, Sharon K., and Weldon F. Zenger. *Strategies and Techniques for Teaching: With Lesson Design and Micro-Teaching Guidelines.* Saratoga, CA: R & E Publishers, 1990.